STO

THE MONTANA RAILROAD

alias: The Jawbone
also known as
THE CHICAGO, MILWAUKEE, ST. PAUL
AND PUGET SOUND
and
THE CHICAGO, MILWAUKEE, ST. PAUL
AND PACIFIC RAILROAD
and finally as
THE MILWAUKEE ROAD

By Don Baker

Published by Fred Pruett
2928 Pearl
Boulder, Co, 80301

CONTENTS

THE JAWBONE

He rambled to Montana, he went
from town to town;
At last he got aboard the "Jaw-Bone" bound
for Lewistown;
He was three days going to Harlowton and
four days to Ubet;
And that was about a week ago and
he hasn't reached here yet.

CHORUS

Oh, didn't he ramble, ramble
He rambled all around, in and out of
the town.
Oh, didn't he ramble ramble,
He rambled til the snowdrift cut him down.

There was a man in Lewistown who
worked upon the grade.
Contracted all the summer long and many
miles he made.
His work was all completed, he was
ready to go home.
But he had to wait a week or two upon the
old Jawbone.

He rambled to the station here, he
wanted to leave the town;
He asked the agent for the train, - his
face began to frown;
The agent says, "I am sorry, but I do not
know;
No doubt a few miles out from here it is
buried in the snow."

The old stage that done the work for
twenty years or more,
Delivered mail in Lewistown right at the
office door.
But when the Jawbone took its
place, it had to take a back seat;
But the people now are well aware that
the old coach couldn't be beat.

She rambled through the hills and
lanes and in the snow so deep;
But when her time was up in Lewistown she surely in would creep

There certainly was an awful time
when Christmas, it was here,
And those who got their Christmas mail
for the old coach they must cheer.

The superintendent, he's all right, but
he don't own the road,
And if he could to tell the truth, I
don't think he would.
He travels up and down the road telling
those he meets
That by and by the old Jawbone will
sure be hard to beat.

You've got to be a rambler and know
a thing or two
When you go aboard the Jawbone
with Lewistown in view,
You may be ditched, - in other words,
delayed a week or two,
For the engines old can't stand the cold
like they could when they were new.

The old Jawbone has been making
time - the fact we can't deny-
Was running pretty regular, and at
times she tried to fly;
But the same old thing occurred again,
and there's no use to buck,
For somewhere out along the line in a
snow bank she is stuck.

The Jawbone is a rambler that rambles
everywhere,
The way it gets to Lewistown would make
a Christian swear.
It rambles into a snowdrift some place
along the line,
So - the chances are that she'll get here this
time.

From the Lewiston *New Argus*
(author unknown)

A 1903 map of the Montana Railroad

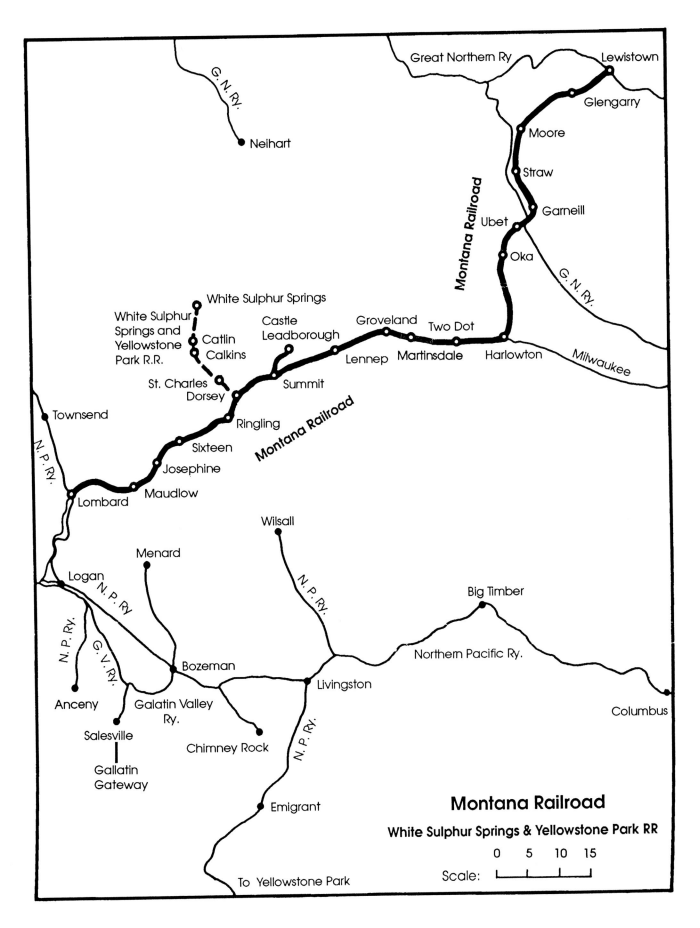

Neihart

Lewistown

Great Northern Ry

Glengarry

Moore

Straw

Garneill

Ubet

Oka

G. N. RY.

Montana Railroad

White Sulphur Springs

White Sulphur
Springs and
Yellowstone
Park R.R.

Catlin
Calkins

Castle
Leadborough

Groveland

Two Dot

Milwaukee

St. Charles
Dorsey

Summit

Lennep

Martinsdale

Harlowton

Townsend

Ringling

Montana Railroad

Sixteen

Josephine

N. P. RY.

Maudlow

Lombard

Wilsall

Menard

Logan

N. P. RY.

Big Timber

N. P. RY.

N. P. RY.

G. V. RY.

Bozeman

Northern Pacific Ry.

Anceny

Galatin Valley
Ry.

Livingston

Columbus

Salesville

Chimney Rock

N. P. RY.

Gallatin
Gateway

Emigrant

Montana Railroad

White Sulphur Springs & Yellowstone Park RR

0   5   10   15

Scale:

To Yellowstone Park

Montana Railroad

Timetable dated October 8, 1908 in the Official Guide.

#103	#6	Station	Miles	#3	#106
	11;20 AM	Lombard	0	2;30 PM	
	11;26	Crane	3	2;23	
		Deer Park	8		
		Goodell	11		
		Maudlow	14		
	12;10 PM	Josephine	19	1;34	
		Canyon	24		
	12;44	Sixteen	27	1;03	
	12;55	Fanalulu	30	12;55	
	1;07	Minden	36	12;46	
		Leader	37		
	1;30	Dorsey	45	12;25	
	1;55	Summit	49	12;10	
		Dublin	52		
	2;26	Lennep	60	11;38 AM	
	2;44	Groveland	66	11;16	
	2;53	Martinsdale	70	11;06	
	3;22	Two Dot	82	10;32	
10;05 AM	4;05	Harlowton	94	10;00	3;40 PM
10;40	4;40	Oka	107	9;13	3;13
11;02	5;02	Ubet	116	8;46	2;46
11;14	5;14	Garneill	121	8;34	2;34
11;28	5;28	Straw	128	8;16	2;16
11;48	5;48	Moore	138	7;52	1;52
12;08	6;10	Glengarry	148	7;32	1;32
12;35	6;35 PM	Lewistown	157	7;10 AM	1;10 PM

Montana Railroad Company TIME TABLE No. 19

Taking Effect at 12:01 A. M. Monday, June 3, 1907

For the government of employees only.   The Company reserves the right to vary therefrom as circumstances may require.

EAST BOUND									WEST BOUND	
FIRST CLASS No. 22 PASSENGER DAILY, EXCEPT SUNDAY		W- Water C - Cool Y - Wye	Station Number		TIME TABLE No. 19 JUNE 3, 1907 SUCCEEDING No. 18		Capacity of Sidings		FIRST CLASS No. 21 PASSENGER DAILY EXCEPT SUNDAY	
LV.	9:30 A. M.	W.C.Y	0	0	LOMBARD N	157	63	Dispr. Agt.	4:00 P. M.	
	9:57	W.	9	9	DEEP PARK	148	10		3:31	"
	10:12		14	14	MAUDLOW	143	20		3:15	"
F	10:24		18	18	JOSEPHINE	139	14		3:01	"
F	10:36		21	21	BAKERS SIDING	136	10		2:51	"
F	10:36		22	22	BAKERS	135			2:47	"
F	10:51		24	24	CANYON SPUR	133	8		2:23	"
F	11:01	W. 2.5 ml's east	27	27	SIXTEEN	130	11		2:09	"
F	11:28		36	36	MINDEN	121	14		1:44	"
	11:55 A. M.	C.Y.	45	45	DORSEY	112	14		1:19	"
	12:01 P. M.	W.	47	47	SPUR No. 47	110	10			
Arr.	12:11 "				SUMMIT	108	40	Dep.	12:59	
Dep.	12:31 "	Y. C.	49	49				Arr.	12:39	
	12:36 " mts. 21		50	50	LEADBORO JCT.	107			12:36	"
	12:46		52	52	DUBLIN	105	10		12:28	"
	1:08 "		60	60	LENNEP	97	14		12:04 P. M.	
F	1:29 "	W. 1.5 ml's west	66	66	GROVELAND	91	7		11:45 A. M.	
	1:41 "	Y.	70	70	MARTINSDALE	87	33		11:32	"
	2:11 "	W.	82	82	TWODOT	75	16		11:02	"
	2:48 " 1 mile east	C. Y.	95	95	HARLOWTON	62	50		10:25	"
F	3:17 "		107	107	OKA	50	10		9:55	"
	3:39 "	W. Y.	116	116	UBET	41			9:32	"
	3:53 "		121	121	GARNEILL	36	30		9:19	"
	4:12 "		128	128	STRAW	29	12		9:03	"
	4:38 "	W.	138	138	MOORE	19	30		8:37	"
F	5:03 "		148	148	GLENGARRY	9	12		8:12	"
Arr.	5:30 P. M.	W. C. Y.	157	157	LEWISTOWN	0	30		7:50 A. M.	

SPECIAL RULES.

Trains will not exceed schedule time descending mountain grades. Engineers will exercise special care and caution...snow around sharp curves and bluffs. East-bound trains will not exceed ten miles per hour Leadboro Junction switch to Dublin.West-bound trains will not exceed ten miles per hour from Summit to Spur No. 47 and from Canyon Spirt Bridge and eight miles per hour Bridge 58 to Mile Post 22West-bound freight trains will not exceed fifteen miles per hour from Dorsey to Lombard, without special order.Swith at Leadboro Juntion will be kept locked for main line.

Extra freight trains will not carry passengers except on special permission from the Superintendent. All employees of the Operating Department will be governed by the general rules of the Northern Pacific book of rules which may be had on application at office of Superintendent. All trains will run with the utmost caution and watchfulness wherever the new work is under way. No train having the right to the road must leave any station where it should meet a train until five minutes after its time and it must be observed at every succeding station until it shall have met the expected train. The five minutes are allowed for the variation of watches and must not be used by either train.

Number 21 has right over Number 22

F-- Trains stop on Flag or to leave passengers

* -- Trains do not stop.

N-- Night Office.

LOCATION OF MAIL CRANES

Maudlow, 8 telephone poles West of M.P. 14

Bakers,	22	"	"	"	"	"	"	20
Sixteen,	15	"	"	"	"	"	"	28
Lennep,	5	"	"		"	"	"	59
Oka,	-	"	"		"	"	"	108

9

ACKNOWLEDGEMENTS & THANKS

An historic accounting of what went before is dependent upon many sources. Thanks are due to the many friends, both old and new, who helped by providing data, pictures, and stories about the building of what at the time was considered a great railroad. At least by Montana's standards, it was a railroad that altered the course of history among many towns and villages, feeding the dreams of others besides Richard Austin Harlow.

The author wishes to thank the following:

• Jim and Faye Fuller for gathering snapshots and opening doors in Meagher County, Montana.
• Warren McGee for pictures and information regarding Lombard.
• Gordon Irion for sharing his wealth of information regarding the railroads and allowing me to use his many resources.
• Lee and Phil Rostad for copying many pages of the *Meagher County Republican* and the *Rocky Mountain Husbandman*. And then granting permission to use parts of the story that she wrote for *Montana Magazine*.
• Bill Wilkerson for copies of his drawing of the electric motors that were used on the Milwaukee.
• Ken Clark for the use of *Pacific Ways*, a story entitled "The Electric Way Across the Mountains."
• The Milwaukee Railroad Company for the use of their *Brief History of The Milwaukee Railroad*.
• Karl Zimmerman's *The Milwaukee Road Under Wire*.
• Vern and Esther Tronnes for their considerable resources of material.
• The Harlowton Women's Club, publishers of *Yesteryears and Pioneers*.
• John Willard.
• Clarence "King" Wilson.
• The Billings Public Library.
• And dear Blanche, my spouse, for encouragement and every kind of help.

PREFACE

The Milwaukee Railroad has answered to several different names in its lifetime. In its last days in Montana east of Miles City it was known as "The Milwaukee." This ill-fated line was also known as the "The Chicago, Milwaukee, St. Paul and Pacific Railroad" and when it was built through the Dakotas and Montana in its drive toward the Pacific extension it was called "The Chicago, Milwaukee, St. Paul and Puget Sound Railroad."

An obscure local railroad was purchased by the Milwaukee during its expansion to the Pacific coast. This 157-mile railroad was called the Montana Railroad, running between Lombard and Lewistown, Montana. The owners of the fledgling railroad tried their best to bring respectability to the Montana Railroad, but the locals persisted in calling it "The Jawbone."

The Milwaukee also furnished the rolling stock for a twenty-one mile short line that was named "The White Sulphur Springs and Yellowstone Park Line." It connected to the Milwaukee at Ringling and extended to White Sulphur Springs. Its expansive name hinted at the hyperbole that great plans demanded. The original plans called for this to be a "Park to Park" railroad.

Nothing remains of these ghost railroads but the traces of a roadbed, a few bridges, stock-loading pens, a few signals and depots at Martinsdale, Ringling, and White Sulphur Springs. The last one, as well as Great Northern coach #902, was used in the set for the movie *Heartland*.

The stark, empty buildings that were once roundhouses, depots and power stations are riddled by broken windows. The right-of-way is overrun with weeds, including some of the most noxious in Montana's landscape. Entire communities were abandoned to the elements as the early day optimism collapsed because of competition, better highways, airline travel, and the agricultural communities' shrinking needs for services nearby.

There were those who forecast this fate when it was built because of the Panama Canal construction and others who didn't believe that the Pacific Northwest could support a third transcontinental line. There are as many different reasons given for its collapse as there are people who had an interest in it. Management blames unionism and union members blame inept management. It does seem irresponsible to abandon electric motive power on the eve of the Arab oil embargo and escalating diesel fuel cost.

But my purpose is not to judge or assign blames. I'm only interested in preserving in some small way the history of a railroad that is nearly forgotten. It is already gone.

Only the most devout railroad fan will fully appreciate the absence of the Jawbone and its contribution; it is for that railfan that I have written this book.

Don Baker

11

INTRODUCTION

Richard Austin Harlow died at the age of seventy-three in Rosslyn, Virginia. His obituary reads, "The construction of the Montana Railroad during such trying times has always been considered one of the remarkable romances in railroad building."

The Montana was Harlow's crowning achievement. The actual construction took place over a period of thirteen years, extending initially from Lombard, Montana, on the Missouri River where it joined the just built Northern Pacific to Leadborough, high in the Castle Mountains. The original plans called for it to be built to neighboring Castle, Montana, a booming silver camp, home to more than a thousand miners prospectors, merchants, and speculators. But the silver panic of 1893 and resulting depression ended the Castle dream. Harlow took a deep breath and extended the fledgling line into Merino and thence northerly to Lewistown.

It is a story of adversity, financial leverage, and remarkably good luck. The Montana Railroad was sold to the Chicago, Milwaukee and Puget Sound Railroad in 1910. Harlow was thereby relieved of his enormous debt to the Northern Pacific and mortgage obligation to James J. Hill, the empire builder. He retired to his home in Virginia after closing the $3,500,000 sale.

CHAPTER I

Castle, Montana

During the last twenty years of the nineteenth century, Montana Territory attracted propectors, opportunist, ne'er-do-wells, stockmen, lumbermen, freighters, merchants, and entrepreneurs. Each of them played a role as the territory opened to settlement and civilization took root in the valleys and along the rivers of what would soon become a state.

Hundreds of legends were born in mining, agriculture, and commerce. The Plummer gang, the Stuart brothers, the Copper Kings, Martin Maginnis, Thomas Meagher, and various community builders left their brands on the past. Opportunities nodded to the continuing string of new arrivals, who struck out in every direction exploring and exploiting mineral prospects, tall virgin timber, and the waving grasses.

The Northern Pacific Railroad contractors drove the golden spike in 1883 at Gold Creek, Montana, joining the west and east bound contracts. This introduced a dependable Chicago to Pacific Coast railroad to the Great Plains and Rocky Mountains of the Northwest. Butte swiftly became the queen city of the northern Rockies, a community of ethnic varieties and nearly a hundred thousand people. It dominated the territory's political and economic scene.

Copper became the king of the hill astraddle the continental divide at Butte. The ugly grayish ore fed the insatiable appetites of the nation's electrical generators. The Northern Pacific was very much a party to the continuing success of the "Richest Hill on Earth."

The Northern Pacific also introduced a new era to stock grazing on the northern plains. Livestock no longer had to be trailed-back to the warmer climate of the south after a summer's grazing season. The railhead was readily available to the stockmen, drovers, and cowboys. Fences were rare, but a new era was at hand.

Hundreds of mining camps came into being throughout the western spine of the mountains. Silver and gold strikes attracted the forty-niners before they were drawn to the Alaskan rush ten to fifteen years later.

H.H. Barnes discovered the first deposits of silver in the Castle Mountains in 1882. Just a year later, the Hensley brothers, Lafe, Isaac, and John, made significant finds of lead and silver in what quickly became the Cumberland District along Allebaugh Creek. Mining camps named Bonanza, Giant, Smith's, Blackhawk, and Robinson exploded throughout the Castles and people flocked to the newly discovered finds. Yet another boom was in the making while the town of Castle was being born.

Castle, Montana.

Jim & Fay Fuller Collection

Jim & Fay Fuller Collection

Main Street, Castle, Montana.

Castle hummed with activity and industry, rivaling White Sulphur Springs as Meagher County's foremost city. Civic leaders incorporated the town and developed an electrical system as well as a water network. There were nine retail establishments, banks, barbers, butchers, brothels, two hotels, fourteen saloons, newspapers, three smelters, and a Vigilance Committee. Calamity Jane Canary became one of the community's foremost citizens for a brief while attempting to dry out and go straight before she moved on to Lewistown and Billings.

The *Whole Truth* became the city's foremost newspaper, constantly pleading with the power structure to enlarge upon the economic base of Castle. The county seat of governance had recently been relocated from Diamond City to White Sulphur Springs. Castle's denizens demanded that their community be considered as the logical candidate for a new county seat. The city had a population in excess of 2,000, and it was growing fast. The publisher of the *Whole Truth* commented, "This place is becoming

such an active place that it will soon be necessary to add days to the weekly calendar. There is just too much going on."

What had been the Carroll Trail served the mining camps. Freighters and stagecoaches delivered ore and passengers to Helena by way of Diamond City and Canyon Ferry. White Sulphur Springs succeeded Brewer's Hot Springs as a way station where passengers and drivers could get an evening of rest and a refreshing bath before the next day's journey to Helena.

All of Meagher County was booming in 1885. The diggings were producing from Maiden and Kendall to Copperopolis to Castle. Montana was enjoying unprecedented prosperity.

Restless men in the East left the security of families and friends and headed for the untamed mountain states. Professionals as well as those seeking an escape from a past found their ways to Montana. Doctors and lawyers in particular were needed wherever people congregated to injure and then repair themselves. A young lawyer from

Ron and Cheryl Schrader

Main Street, Castle, Montana, 1890

Chicago was among those who hung his shingle on an office door in Montana.

Richard Austin Harlow graduated from law school at Northwestern University in Evanston, Illinois, with the class of 1885. His health was such that the drier climate of Montana attracted him, and in 1886 he moved to Helena to begin his practice of law.

Harlow was soon caught up in the promotional activities of the territory's business community and its most prominent citizens. Helena was rapidly filling its ranks with millionaires. Business proposals and social activities occupied many of his leisure hours. Harlow moved comfortably among other business and professional people in Helena and soon was dealing in real estate ventures as a sideline. He eventually became intensely interested in railroading, while the Northern Pacific built branch lines, the Utah and Northern extended to Butte, and dreams of empire building entered most every tycoon's conversation. Eventually, Charles Broadwater built the Montana Central and

Samuel Hauser promoted and built the Helena Northern. Harlow's recollections from Chicago suggested to him that railway transportation would be the wave of the future as the western outback bacame settled, developed, and exploited. He visualized hubs extending in each direction from Helena, much as the rails were built in every direction from Chicago. Harlow became more and more occupied with his obsession until in 1891 he hired W.A. Havin, an experienced railroad construction engineer, to commence preliminary workings east of Helena.

The ambitious railroad builder to be was encouraged by the publicity accorded Jim Hill's Great Northern drive across the prairies. It motivated the shakers and doers in Helena and environs to accomplish their more local efforts. Harlow made the long trip to New Jersey to persuade a frequent Helena visitor to throw his financial weight behind this new idea. J.P. Whitney, an industrialist from Glassboro, New Jersey, became the primary financial angel for Harlow's dreams.

Meagher County Historical Society

Cumberland Mine near shafthouse, 1888.

Cumberland Mine near Castle,   **Meagher County Historical Society.**

Yellowstone smelter at Castle.

Helena's business community also mustered pledges of material and real estate valued at $200,000 to initate the new east-bound railroad. Harlow had every intention of making use of those incentives to build his new railroad when he incorporated it in 1893, naming himself as president, Havin as chief engineer, and William Guchs as treasurer of the Montana Midland Railroad.

The community of Castle had petitioned the Northern Pacific to extend its line in their direction from Livingston since railway service was much superior to the oxen trails that were then used to haul ore, but their requests were denied. However, Harlow's more and more frequent visits to Castle convinced him of the feasibility of a line direct to the East Helena smelter and fed the fuels of optimism in Castle. Both the *Whole Truth* and *Rocky Mountain Husbandman* applauded the decision to extend rails to the hustling camps of Meagher County.

Havin's survey recommended a route that proceeded from Helena to Canyon Ferry, where a bridge would be built across the Missouri River. It approximated what had been the Carroll Trail to Diamond City, the Smith River valley, White Sulphur Springs, Copperopolis, and Castle. Dependable and inexpensive transportation assured the reworking of the Confederate Gulch diggings at Diamond City, from where prospectors had already left in search of easier diggings.

Construction commenced from Helena to East Helena during October of 1893 with plans for the building of the Missouri River bridge in November.

In the meantime, Harlow organized another railroad company with plans to expand to Whitehall through the Boulder valley and the area's many mining camps.

But financial panic resulted from the repeal of the Sherman Silver Purchase Act in 1892. The value of silver dropped by half to sixty-five cents an ounce, resulting in a total collapse of the silver mining business throughtout the Rocky Mountain West.

Harlow's grandiose plans went entirely awry. Just five miles of grading had been started when the construction aborted.

Castle, Montana, 1985   **Don Baker**

Castle, Montana, 1985.   Don Baker

Don Baker   Castle, Montana, 1985

The Montana Midland ceased to exist, as did the $200,000 incentive. There were never to be any additional gift moneys available for the building of Harlow's railroad. He went back to the practice of law until such time as the country's life improved.

Castle went into eclipse, with hundreds of people leaving for a more promising future. Mines were abandoned and store fronts boarded against the weather. A few hearty optimists remained to gather the pieces that remained and await the arrival of the hoped for railroad. Those who left squatted on land in the foothills of the Crazies and the Belts, taking up careers in stock raising and freighting.

Don Baker   **Castle, Montana, 1985.**

CHAPTER II

The Contracts

Undeterred by the failure of the Montana Midland venture, Harlow organized a successor company called the Montana Railroad Company. The articles of incorporation, dated May 26, 1895, named Cutler Whitney of New York, William Fuchs, A.G. Lombard, John Wilson, and M.S. Gunn as incorporators, with Gunn named the president. Those articles further stated that the line would extend into Gallatin, Meagher, and Jefferson counties from its Helena base. The Montana was incorporated for $3,500,000 in shares priced at $100 each. A.G. Lombard was appointed chief engineer and his predecessor, Havin of the illfated Montana Midland, was employed as a consultant.

This new Montana was to run northeasterly from Helena to the Missouri River at Spokane Creek, thence southeasterly to the mouth of Sixteen Mile Creek. This was so named because it was sixteen miles from where the Gallatin, Jefferson, and Madison rivers joined to form the Missouri.

Work was commenced immediately upon incorporation at what was then called the Sixteen Mile Division. Four contracts were negotiated by Harlow. The contractors who had agreed to do the grading work accepted notes secured by bonds in lieu of cash for their work. These time checks were discounted by innkeepers and merchants in amounts ranging from fifteen to twenty-five percent. The second contract involved the Cumberland Mining Company. They agreed to exchange 7,000 tons of ore lying in their dump for railroad bonds. The third called for the East Helena Smelting Company to pay $150,000 in cash for the ore when it was delivered to the smelter. And the last contract was negotiated with the Northern Pacific Railroad. The N.P. agreed to sell rails, spikes, fittings, locomotives, and rolling stock for which they accepted notes secured by bonds. In return, the Montana guaranteed the Northern Pacific traffic and freight at Sixteen Mile Junction, soon to be named Castle Junction in a justified wave of optimism. This last contract negated the need to independently build a line to Helena. The Northern Pacific had that connection up and running.

There was soon concern, however, when the Helena *Independent* reported that the construction contract was cancelled with the Heidenrach Construction Company, a Chicago railroad builder experienced in such matters. The *Independent* speculated that the great plans were doomed. Harlow immediately notified the newspapers of the state that "such was not the case. There was a

23

Sixteen Mile Creek, in Sixteen Mile Canyon, 1985   **Don Baker**

Don Baker   **Sixteen Mile Creek, in Sixteen Mile Canyon, 1985**

misunderstanding with the Heidenrach people and we did cancel their contract. We have no intention of dropping the project though."

The Montana hired the contractors who had successfully bid the Montana Midland job two years previously. They were John Brady, William Quinn, Matt Viads, B.J. Townsend, and W.H. Green. Green had died in the meantime, but his widow executed the contracts. The responsibilities were divided and called for developing the grade, erecting the bridges, and laying the ties and rails.

The contractors employed for the Sixteen Mile Canyon job endured their own kind of hell. Townsend took on the job because he was then unemployed. He had no other work on the drawing board and was completely without money. He quickly moved his equipment and forty horses to the construction site. Harlow had promised him food, tobacco, clothing, blasting powder, and blacksmithing services. He was to be paid in time checks that would eventu-

ally be redeemable at par. Townsend's son, a lad of sixteen years, was thawing dynamite at the job site while working with his father. He carelessly took the cover off of a box of caps and set it a few feet from the fire. A spark ignited the caps, badly mangling the boy's hand and resulting in the loss of all but one finger. He also lost sight in one eye.

William Quinn also contracted for the roadbed work but eventually worked at providing ties. There were four saw mills set up higher on the stream and logs were floated to the tie plant. The lack of cash and constant worry contributed to his decision to commit suicide on the job.

The principal earthmoving devices were wheeled scrapers, pulled by four horses or mules. When the scraper was loaded, a two horse team pulled it to where the load was needed. Winter all too soon closed in on the job and the frozen, snow-covered earth resisted all attempts to move it.

Lombard assured the state's newspapers that progress was coming on nicely.

Don Baker

Sixteen Mile Creek, in Sixteen Mile Canyon, 1985.

"We'll employ 5,000 men and several hundred teams this summer and we'll hire anyone who shows up to work on the lower twelve miles of Sixteen Mile Creek. We should have this portion of the line in running order before the snow flies."

During the winter a crew of a hundred men worked at the box canyon, three miles from the construction camp at the village of Sixteen. They were building a five percent grade over the top.

The canyon job was incredibly difficult. The state of the art in railroad building was hard work, man and animal power.

Fifty-eight bridges were to be built during the first eighteen miles. The roadbed paralleled the creek, climbing a steady one percent grade to the box canyon. The builders encountered hostile ranchers and angry rattlesnakes during the warm months of July and August and faced the prospect of a long, cold winter trapped in an unfriendly environment.

Lombard's rosy projections were doomed from the start. There were simply too many obstacles lying in the path of construction.

The Montana was festering with problems, expecially those associated with money. Harlow paid his first bills, totaling $10,000, on July 20, 1895. He exhausted the cash in the account within an hour and the remaining payees were advised to return the following Monday. Bills were paid from that date forward with warrants.

Following the experience of the cancelled contract with Heidenrach, the Helena *Independent* would be expected to be wary of Harlow's dealings. Yet they reported after that first payday that "the Montana is in fine shape financially."

Wages for workers were advertised at $2.00 per day, less $5.00 per week for board and room. Teams were paid at the rate of $3.00 daily for both the driver and the team, with the driver furnishing his own horses and doubletrees. The construction company furnished the scrapers, feed for the teams, and did all of the blacksmithing. Payment was made in time checks, which usually averaged 75¢ on the dollar, "but certainly worth more upon completion of the railroad," the *Husbandman* reported. The grading contract was completed for the first twenty-five miles as autumn ended late in October. The bridge contractor in the canyon had also completed driving piles for the tenth of the fifty-eight bridges across Sixteen Mile Creek.

The early settlers along the Montana's right-of-way filed a lawsuit at this time attempting to halt further construction. Robert Sutherlin, the editor of the *Rocky Mountain Husbandman*, lamented, "We've learned with some surprise that some of the settlers along Sixteen Mile Creek have commenced legal proceedings to restrain the progress of the Montana Railroad. This is to be regretted since the road is an absolute necessity and private interest is often compelled to yield to the public good. It is true that the settlers should be paid for the damages that they sustain ... the railroad must come in spite of all the opposition of the landowners."

The Sutherlin brothers had become convinced by virtue of frequent visits by Harlow and Lombard to their favorite town that the Montana would someday serve White Sulphur Springs. The fact that its projected route skirted the county seat by eighteen miles was of little moment. It was apparent to them that the foremost city in central Montana would eventually be served by this progressive railroad.

Montana's legendary winters commenced in November of 1895, dashing all of Harlow's and Lombard's predictions. The swirling snow and frozen ground slowed construction to a walk, and the crews were reduced to those in the box canyon. Their pay was cut in half.

The state's newspapers were full of rumors regarding the Montana Railroad during the cold, long winter. The most persistent speculation involved the Burlington Railroad, which terminated at Billings. It seemed logical for the Burlington to extend westerly to meet the Montana.

Other rumors reported in the newspapers had the Northern Pacific branching from east of Billings to pick up the coal fields of the lower Musselshell River and extending west to meet the Montana at Summit, at the top of the saddle separating the Castle from the Crazy mountain ranges.

Because of the doubts, suspicions, and rumors upon rumors, White Sulphur Springs became convinced that the railroad would not terminate at Castle, but instead would build east from Summit following the Musselshell River to Merino, where it would build on north to Lewistown and the Judith Basin country.

H.H. Barnes, in a statement in the *Whole Truth*, expressed his certainty that "Castle will once again be the most prosperous city in the county and undoubtedly the place for this county's capitol." The remark didn't endear Barnes to the powers of White Sulphur Springs, nor did it accomplish anything that would restore Castle to its former

glory. The depression worsened during the mid-nineties. The decade may have been "gay" elsewhere, but not in the silver mining districts of Montana. Most of those camps, including Castle, were engrossed with survival.

The pervasive gloom didn't weaken Harlow's resolve. The pile of ore at the Cumberland's dump in Leadborough and the payment for it to be rendered by the East Helena refinery, combined with his stubborn nature, pushed the contracts ahead.

Deep canyon snow added to the woes of maintenance and the expense of construction. The crews were reduced to only those at the top of the canyon where a five percent grade was being conquered. Neither Lombard nor Harlow was frightened by the project's enormous appetite for money. They expressed complete optimism whenever they

Warren McGee collection.

Jawbone construction in Sixteen Mile Canyon.

were given the opportunity, and Lombard predicted, "the rails will reach Castle before the Fourth of July, 1896. The hundreds of cars of ore at Castle combined with the smelter contract was the Montana's certain way of overcoming the substantial debt load that had accumulated in six months. The history of railroad building was not significantly different in Montana than it had been elsewhere. It may well have frightened lesser men.

Harlow, in a later personal interview remarked, "We had a frightful time getting supplies up Sixteen Mile Creek that winter. A team and a wagon had to travel sixty miles to get from the lower to the upper end of the box canyon, which is scarcely a half mile long. A four horse team left from Toston and landed without a pound of oats in the wagon. It had been caught in a blizzard and the driver had to feed all of the oats to his horses. We had trouble with labor, with our engi- neering parties and it seemed with everything with which we came in contact. Trouble was the normal condition. The owners of the ranches held us up with shotguns and hesitated to sell us supplies, fearing that they wouldn't get paid."

The Montana Railroad was quickly nicknamed the "Jawbone" as a result of Harlow's nagging financial problems, the leverage that he'd achieved with his construction contracts, and his inability to meet his payroll. He talked all of his creditors into accepting time and discounts, becoming very skilled at "jawboning" the railroads's financial obligations. The nickname stuck throughout the existence of the Montana Railroad and there are few native Montanans who fail to recall the Jawbone's travail. It did, however, achieve a life of its own by virture of Harlow's and Lombard's unbounded enthusiasm and optimism.

CHAPTER III

An Operating Railroad

Construction progress was faithfully reported by the *Rocky Mountain Husbandman* during the spring and summer of 1896. The crews were within twelve miles of Castle and the Castle *Whole Truth* predicted that the grading would be completed by July 15. The bridge crews were doing "nicely." It was anticipated that that phase of the contract would be completed by the time the rails arrived at Castle Junction. The erection of the trestle across Warm Springs Creek, just four miles from Leadborough, plagued the builders. It was fifty four feet high and two hundred feet long. The structure was buffeted by constant winds during the summer and early autumn, keeping the laborers in constant fear of falling. The progress of the solid wooden construction was slow beyond all imaginings.

Boardroom discussions undoubtedly focused on the shrinking production of the Cumberland District and declining population of Castle. The only genuine need for the Leadborough extension was to pick up the ore there and transport it to East Helena, where the Montana would get paid sufficient monies to liquidate some of its debt. No plans were made to extend the rails beyond the ore dump despite the Sutherlin brother's weekly pleas to include White Sulphur Springs in the Montana's plans for railroad building.

Finally, a celebration occurred on November 25, 1896, when the Montana's completion was hosted by the Moore brothers in Leadborough and toasted by the entire community. Witnessing the arrival of a genuine train was described as "a sight for sore eyes."

Despite the pleadings of the Sutherlins there was never any serious consideration given to building to Castle, Copperopolis, or White Sulphur Springs.

Harlow announced plans to immediately commence construction east of Summit with Merino as his destination. The Leadborough branch was destined to play a minor role in the Montana Railroad plans and a relatively brief one at that. The depression that had settled over the mountain country deepened with each year, but John Nesbitt, the primary bridge builder for the Montana, settled in Castle to take up silver and lead mining. Others took up claims in waves of high hopes. The product was still there and now freight was available to the industry. Yet Castle continued to decline with each passing year, and fewer and fewer passengers rode the railroad. The peak production year was 1895 when 1,800 mines were being worked, just one year before the arrival of the Jawbone.

The lawsuit against the railroad by settlers in 1895 was gradually being settled, with only the Foster Sheep Company insisting upon condemnation proceedings. Harlow and his investors were kept occupied with such matters even after the completion of what they had hoped would be a very profitable and feasible railroad.

The Montana advertised its schedule throughout its territory. It ran a mixed passenger and freight service daily, except Sunday, leaving Castle Junction at eight in the morning and Leadborough at two in the afternoon. The ride from Leadborough to Dorsey was one of forty-five minutes, almost all of it downhill. Good dining and sleeping accommodations were available at Castle Junction, where Billy Kee was owner and host of the hotel.

After the construction was completed, the next step in running a railroad was the creation of an Operations Department. Harlow appointed F. Green as that departments manager. Shortly afterwards, the town of Castle Junction was renamed Lombard in honor of the man who battled the elements and all of the longest odds to build the Jawbone. A.G. Lombard remained as the railroad's chief engineer and substantial shareholder.

Ron and Cheryl Schrader collection

Tearing the trestle down between Summit and Leadborough, 1904

Montana Railroad trestle over Warm Springs Creek, 1904.
Meagher County Historical Society

Ron & Cheryl Schrader collection
Dorsey, 1907

Dorsey, 1907
Lombard, Montana. Billy Kee's hotel and general store and postoffice.

Meagher County Historical Society
Warren McGee collection

Billy Kee, proprieter of the hotel in Lombard, and family.

CHAPTER IV

The Extension

White Sulphur Spring's frustration persisted because the area's mineral wealth was being wasted and its tourist potential could never be realized without adequate transportation. Its hot water spa was compared to those of Baden Baden in Germany, but only a few weary, dust-covered travelers enjoyed them. The Sutherlins were certain that the city would become an oasis of 10,000 people if only dependable and scheduled transportration was available to it. The remnants of the Carroll Trail were not sufficient to give White Sulphur Springs the necessary boost, but Harlow's railroad offered that longheld hope.

The Montana Railroad functioned throughout its first year without a steady and reliable income. The mining boom never did return to the district, and Castle's viable lifetime was but a decade. Only a few shipments of wool were transported from Leadborough after the ore dump had been removed.

The train that arrived in Leadborough to recover the pile of ore lying at the dump near the depot was accompanied by a crew of men shoveling snow the entire way from Dorsey, a distance approaching ten miles. Lombard and Campbell brought the train into the station and to the waiting crowd. By

May 26, 1895, 156 cars of ore had been hauled from Leadborough to the smelter at East Helena. Most of the incoming tonnage, estimated at two million tons, was destined eventually for White Sulphur Springs. Almost none of it was bound for Castle.

Despite the adversity surrounding the Montana, every attempt was made to put a pretty face on it. The railroad sponsored a ride from Leadborough to Summit, thence to Dorsey and down Sixteen Mile Canyon. It was a heralded event during the spring of 1897, and R.N. Sutherlin was ecstatic with the scenery and the convenience of Harlow's new business.

The Montana's problems persisted with a minimum of cash flow. Harlow liquidated some of his debt with the ore that his railroad carried to East Helena, but the red ink remained on the books. During the spring floods of 1898, the entire roadbed through the canyon washed out. The entire canyon division had to be rebuilt. There was little doubt that dramatic steps would have to be taken to bring to fruition the dreams of a profitable railroad.

J.P. Whitney had reached the bottom of his financial pockets. He wanted out, forcing Harlow to seek a new source of financing. Extending the line from Summit to

Martinsdale became Harlow's new obsession, but he didn't have operating capital sufficient to run what he had already built.

A statement in the Castle *Whole Truth* by H.H. Barnes complained, "The high cost of freight and the outrageous prices that are charged for processing in Helena are more than the industry in this place can afford to pay." Even the stalwart few picking at the remnants of Castle and the Cumberland District diggings were recognizing the writing on the wall. The Montana Railroad couldn't redeem the failing fortunes of the silver camp. The Leadborough extension faded into obscurity.

Again, there was speculation that the Burlington Railroad, which terminated in Billings, would extend west from that place and unite with the Montana. There appears to have been no substance to that rumor, but it did contain a certain amount of prophecy.

Harlow returned to the eastern establishment for a financial transfusion. Henry D. Moore of Haddonfield, New Jersey, became the railroad's latter day financial angel. "He brought money, faith, generosity and confidence into the enterprise," Harlow was quoted as saying.

The abandonment of the Leadborough extension was already apparent when the trackage was begun east of Summit. The railroad was to assume a stock raising and agricultural base from its failed beginnings as an ore and passenger hauler. Martinsdale became its first objective with Big Elk closely behind. There was no doubt in Harlow's mind that the tracks would extend beyond to Merino, a sheep gathering station, as soon as possible and as long as the money held out. It was an enormous job, more ambitious than what most men would consider in light of the state's economy, but Harlow brought a whole new meaning to the word "daring."

Work was begun on the Musselshell Valley extension during the spring of 1899. It began at Summit, the site of the Leadborough cutoff. Moore's entre into the financial schematic enabled Harlow to enter into yet another contract with the Northern Pacific management and James Hill gave Harlow additional leverage that he was to exercise again and again.

Surveyors and construction engineers designed a railroad that disregarded or destroyed irrigation ditches and improvements that ranchers had built in the valley. Disputes began to cloud the Montana's future again as it had in years past.

M.T. Grande refused to remove a barn that he had built some years previously. Rather than move the alignment of the right-of-way, the $2,500 barn had a corner cut away from it for the passage of the trackage. Grande was paid $700 for the inconvenience and damages.

Construction reached Martinsdale during the month of October. The existing town, however, was located two miles from the tracks, so the town was promptly relocated to the railroad. Harlow announced on the date of arrival that Merino was the ultimate goal of the Montana.

He visualized huge clips of wool transported from the Musselshell Valley to Lombard because there were an estimated 200,000 sheep on the surrounding range. This held some promise for the fledgling Montana Railroad to maintain a reliable source of income. The construction continued through the winter, arriving two miles south of Big Elk in March of 1900.

The few people who inhabited Big Elk moved entirely to the new townsite on the railroad. G.R. "Two Dot" Wilson, owner of the ".." brand, set aside 140 acres of his land to assure that the town had sufficient room to grow. A few buildings were tugged from Big Elk to the new townsite and Wilson built the area's grandest hotel near the station. It was a two-story 36-by 42-foot structure with an additional 30-by 15-foot single-story building attached to it. The Meagher County *Republican* reported, "its appearance is much enhanced by a spacious porch and balcony fronting on the town's main street." Wilson became the town's biggest booster.

Merino was then reached in June 1900, and the new town that grew around the depot and yards was renamed Harlow in honor of the Montana Railroad's founder and builder. The United States Post Office declined the name, claiming that it was too similar to a name already in use in the state, Harlem. The name was then amended to Harlowton.

The promised wool shipments increased each year, reaching two million pounds in its second year of operation.

Harlow looked north toward the Judith Basin and Lewistown. "The advance to Harlowton has put real life into our railroad but even then our receipts over a large part of the year are not sufficient to pay expenses. The onward call to build on to Lewistown cannot be denied."

That construction began in 1902 and was completed at Lewistown in 1903 despite a continuing battle of five months of record snowfall during the winter.

It was at Lewistown that the Montana Railroad finally terminated. The celebration was loud and long on October 31, 1903.

Lewistown was a worthy target for the Montana Railroad. It had seceded from Meagher County and had become the capital of newly created Fergus County in 1895. The new county was diversified farming and ranching country, and several banks located in the city. Additionally, mining camps located in Maiden, Kendall, and Gilt Edge, all looking toward Lewistown for supplies and services.

CHAPTER V

Operational Problems

In operating the Jawbone, there were constant difficulties presented by the equipment, the elements, and the terrain. Following the creek bottom from Lombard to the village of Sixteen assured that flooding would knock out the schedule each spring thaw and summer freshet. The winter storms guaranteed blockage where the winds blew or the canyon walls narrowed.

The rails furnished by the Northern Pacific were not of sufficient strength to handle heavy-duty usage. They were reportedly imported from railyards back east where the need for heavier rail was considerably less than what it was in a cross-country environment. To compound the problem, the entire Montana Railroad was frequently laid on bare ground with little if any ballast or roadbed. And while Lewistown and Lombard are at an approximate identical elevation, the terrain between varies enormously. Judith Gap, a thousand feet higher than Harlowton, is but seventeen miles north of it. This accounts for a substantial grade to reach that elevation with underpowered steam locomotives in a wind belt that has been known to conquer everything in its path, including buffalo. The Gap is also forty-two miles from Lewistown and thirteen hundred feet higher in elevation. There is little relief in traveling the opposite direc-

tion. This stretch of the Montana Railroad became famous for stalling trains, often in the middle of the prairie and not often at sidings or at the convenience of the passengers. Considering two passenger trains per day, it's amazing that more wrecks and casualties didn't occur.

The grade from Harlowton to Martinsdale along the Musselshell River was moderate, but from there west the Montana Railroad was a mountain line. It gradually ascended the saddle between the Castle and Crazy mountain ranges following the south fork of the river. In fifteen miles it reached an elevation of six thousand feet at Summit. From there it spun its crazy way to Sixteen Mile Creek and the jaws of the canyon, dropping another thousand feet in the process.

The character of Sixteen Mile Canyon assured prodigious depths of snow, followed by spring flooding along the creek. Ascending the canyon over the divide into the Smith River country brought the railroad head on into a wind and snow belt. Cuts filled with snow before the first plowing or shoveling was done.

The locomotives leased from the Northern Pacific were old and not powerful enough to handle the grades, wind, and snow. When six-car trains were built at Lombard, it was necessary for them to be halved in order to make it up the grade to Summit. Whatever efficiency or profitability resulted from longer trains was lost in having to split them into two sections. In addition to the feeble locomotives, the other rolling equipment was also leased from the Northern Pacific.

The entire line lay within what is commonly known as the chinook belt. As such it features extremes in climate. Temperatures have risen and fallen by up to fifty degrees within an hour, accompanied by winds of up to eighty miles per hour. Steam locomotives lost much of their efficiency in cold weather and that's all that was available in the early 1900s. Meagher County has had snowstorms during each of the twelve months in some years. Therefore, the Montana developed the reputation of being an unscheduled railroad during the long winter months of central Montana.

Operating a steam locomotive in this capricious climate and rugged terrain was at best backbreaking labor and at its worst impossible. During ideal conditions a tender of coal would easily accommodate the needs between division points, but these ideal conditions were rare. Instead, a booster would be added to the tender between divi-

sion points and the water tank would be tapped as well. These conditions required that a fireman, engineer, and conductor shovel coal into the fire pit. Shoveling up to ten tons of coal in two and half hours under the best of circumstances was hard work. Doubling that in wind and snow conditions guaranteed an aching back.

Still, the Montana Railroad responded to the needs of the country in typical fashion for its day. The Smith and Musselshell River country as well as the Judith Basin and Fergus County became stock country. Sheep and beef cattle became the dominant crop on the open range. The railroad built sheep shearing pens and warehouses over its entire line. Loading pens were built as often as every ten or twelve miles, enabling the freight operation to pick up where the hauling of crude ore had failed.

Small towns emerged at side track intervals named Two Dot, Lennep, Bruno, and Dorsey. Little of them remains. But what does is a testament to the tenacity of Harlow and Lombard.

Any lesser optimists would have surrendered long before the first phases of the project was completed. Only dogged determination and trusting creditors sustained the

A postcard depicts a frequent problem on the Jawbone, 1903.   **Warren McGee collection**

Lombard, Montana, where the Montana Railroad met the Northern Pacific, 1904.

Warren McGee collection

construction and then the operation of the Jawbone. But the light duty rail, inadequate ballast, and primitive equipment combined with the climate to doom the Montana and its successors to a life of misery.

The Northern Pacific leased three 4-4-0's numbered 774, 763, and 800, which were eventually sold to the Montana Railroad. Two 4-6-0's numbered 392 and 394 were also leased from the N.P., but they were returned when the Montana Railroad bought its one 2-8-0 and two 2-6-0's in 1904, 102 and 103 in 1905, with construction numbers 24752, 25643, and 26434. They subsequently became Milwaukee number's 5500, 6004, and 6005. Three other locomotives were number 5, a 4-6-0 built in 1885 by Schenectady and later Milwaukee number 4400; number 22 acquired in 1907 from the Milwaukee, built by the Rhode Island Works in 1881; and number 23, a sister to number 22. This engine was later numbered 4402 and in 1912 was transferred to the Gallatin Valley Railroad. This was the extent of the power equipment

that the Jawbone used in its operation.

The rolling stock, both passenger and freight cars, were also leased from the Northern Pacific. They were entirely of 1880s vintage. The freight cars came out of various N.P. shops and were repainted for the benefit of properly identifying the Montana Railroad as a going concern. They featured the semi-circular logo used by the Northern Pacific. This semi-circular logo was used by only these two Montana lines and the Lehigh Valley and New England Railroad.

Similar coaches were leased to the White Sulphur Springs and Yellowstone Park Railroad when it was built a few years later.

Boxcars during this early period of Montana railroading were thirty feet in length, advertising not only the railroad but the fact that they featured air brakes.

The maintenance and repair of the rolling stock as well as the locomotives was done at the yards in Lombard, the only genuine rail yards on the Montana Railroad. A junction was built there to facilitate the use

Engine 763 at the bottom of Sixteen Mile Canyon after a crash caused by a landslide following the 1925 earthquake.

Warren McGee collection

of the Northern Pacific trackage to East Helena. Lombard became the nerve center for operations and maintenance of the Montana Railroad's equipment. Early into the operation of the Montana Railroad, more than two hundred people resided there, all of whom were dependent upon the Jawbone for employment.

Montana Railroad using Northern Pacific power, 1904.   **Warren McGee collection**

Snow on the Jawbone.   **Phil & Lee Rostad collection**

Dorsey deep under snow, 1904.   **Tom Coburn collection**

Montana Railroad crossing Sixteen Mile Creek at Lombard, 1906.

Warren McGee collection

Warren McGee collection

Montana Railroad facilities at Lombard, 1907.

CHAPTER VI

Passenger Stories

Humorous stories followed the Montana's nagging problems and produced a colorful history. Numerous stories involving the Jawbone survive in the newspapers and diaries of the time.

Traveling as they did through rangeland, trains often encountered grazing livestock on the trackage. An instance was reported in the Lewistown *Argus* of an engine, with whistle blowing and bells ringing, separating a cow from her calf. Typically, the young calf followed the moving object. It took off after the train. At this point, the brakeman came out on the rear platform where two Lewistown men were standing. He tried the air, looked at the calf, said nothing, and went back inside the car. Later he came out and one of the men asked, "Did you notice that calf?"

"Sure did," the brakeman replied. "And for a moment I thought he was going to catch us."

A witty woman, the wife of a district judge, was traveling with another woman, who was accompanied by her teenaged daughter. It was a hot July day and the women, seated near the front of the coach, could look into the baggage coach, where all of its doors were opened. The baggageman had opened the side door in order to get some breeze through the baggage car. At one of the stops the daughter wandered into the baggage car and was invited to have a seat on a folding cot that the baggage man had set up near the door. Calling back to her companions she said, "I've got a berth!" And like a flash the judge's wife quipped, "We've all been here long enough to have one."

The Jawbone's passenger service was ridiculed from one end of the railroad to the other. Weekly newspaper editors persisted in comparing the Montana to the replaced stage teams. Once the Fergus Flyer inadvertently missed a switch and ended in Livingston instead of Lewistown. The embarrassed railroad officials bought an advertisement in the Lewistown *Argus Farmer* that read, "The passenger train scheduled to arrive in Lewistown three weeks ago last Monday will arrive tomorrow evening."

The last surviving engineer for the Jawbone was H.T. O'Donnell, who lived in Three Forks when he was interviewed on July 4, 1965. He was then eighty-one years old. The interview was printed by both the Harlowton *Times* and the Lewistown *News Argus*. Mrs. Francis Denning conducted the interview and wrote the story.

O'Donnell came to Lombard in 1907 to work for the new railroad to Castle.

Workers were promised up to $3.60 a day with the provision that they accept scrip until the road was on a paying basis, presumably in five years. O'Donnell recalls:

"The scrip was good for food and lodging at various stations that sprang up as track was laid. Ties were cut from fir trees along the right-of-way and were laid on the creek bottom. As soon as one portion of track was completed, the promoters would secure a mortgage on it which enabled them to purchase second hand steel from the Northern Pacific to lay the rails. During a spring thaw the water would run completely over the rails which had been laid on the dry creek bottom. To this day, the pilintg set to hold the cuts and fills, may be seen in Sixteen Mile Canyon."

O'Donnell made his first trip as a fireman on the Northern Pacific in June 1902, as engineer in June 1905, and made his first trip as an engineer on the Jawbone in October 1907. At that time there were eighteen Jawbone men who transferred over to the Milwaukee and remained there until they retired. Tom LaFever was the next to last survivor of that group of hardy railroad pioneers.

O'Donnell recalls many hardships endured by workers during the building of the railroad. For instance in 1910, the weather was so cold that the ice froze solidly over the tracks, and when the spring thaw started, the ice broke the bridge piling in Sixteen Mile Canyon. The crew feared that the bridge was unsafe, so the fireman crossed on foot. O'Donnell set the throttle with just enough steam for the engine to cross the bridge, jumped from the cab and let it go. After the engine crossed safely, the fireman hopped in the cab and stopped it.

At one time, it took three months for the crews to remove 230 cars of rock from the tracks. During the process, when they were hauling the debris with small donkey cars, the train with O'Donnell at the throttle rounded a curve and came upon a pyramid of rock on the track. Unable to stop in time, the engine climbed the pile of rock and flipped over and rolled into the creek. The fireman jumped clear of the cab and broke his ankle while O'Donnell rode it down and emerged unharmed.

The G4 engine pulled nine cars and a caboose and was known as a ten wheeler. It carried 140 pounds of steam. The trip from Harlowton to Lewistown took twenty hours in the early part of the century. The last trip that O'Donnell made before his retirement in 1959 took but two hours and forty minutes. The five percent grade had been reduced to one percent.

The passenger train used to stop at Summit, where there was a boardinghouse where the passengers and crews could eat. Meals were fifty cents for "tourists" and twenty-five cents for railroad men. Mr. O'Donnell recalled that a Scandinavian woman ran the boardinghouse and set a bountiful table, and when in about 1907 an official of the railroad stopped for dinner, she produced a check that had been written to her in 1893 to pay board for a worker.

Now that the railroad was comparatively solvent, she wanted her money. The check was made out for five or six dollars, and when the interest was added, computed for the fourteen years, the amount was staggering. She fainted. Being a lady of some bulk, this presented quite a problem for the official.

About this time, the town of Lombard had a floating population of about four hundred with three hundred fifty men working on the construction of the many tunnels in the canyon. The hotel, owned then by Mr. and Mrs. J.N. Klever, boasted forty-nine rooms and a large bunkhouse. O'Donnell met his wife Helen there. She was the Klevers daughter. They married in Helena on November 15, 1911.

The Montana Railroad contributed to the homestead land rush during its short tenure as a local independent railway. M.G. Wright left Nelson, Nebraska, on August 20, 1903, to claim a homestead near the thriving town of Moore, Montana, on the Jawbone line. Moore was named in honor of the last financial angel that Harlow found to complete the Jawbone between Martinsdale and Lewistown via Harlowton. Upon sale of his railroad, Harlow also bought a ranch in the area and briefly settled there until his deal with the Milwaukee finalized and closed.

Wright wrote his story of immigration in the Lewistown *Argus* some years later.

"On September 9 I filed a claim for 160 acres between Moore and Straw. From Lombard to Harlowton, the Jawbone was completed enough to run what they called a train. The passenger coach was a boxcar with a ladder nailed to the side door and benches around the wall for seats.

"The old Northern Pacific junk pile engine could pull about five cars on level track. At the upper end of the Sixteen Mile Canyon they uncoupled and pulled one or two cars to the summit. Passengers detrained and fished while they waited for the engine to come back and get them. At Harlowton we boarded an old stage coach drawn by six mustangs which made better time than the train from Harlowton.

"We left about 11:00 p.m. and arrived at Garneill about 1:00 a.m. I had come dressed for the summer weather that we still enjoyed in Nebraska. W.H. Pack, who was the storekeeper and postmaster asked me, Young man, haven't you an overcoat? When I replied that I didn't he volunteered the use of one of his, a coon skin coat. I asked him why he'd lend it to me when he didn't know if I'd return it or not. He said that he'd loaned it many times and no one had failed to return it yet.

"I filed on my homestead on September 9, 1903 and took the stage at Trout Creek to return to Nebraska to get ready to move out west. I left Nelson, Nebraska on December 12th on an immigrant car. When I arrived at Alliance, I met Perry Black who was also moving to the Judith Basin country in Montana. After four days of travel we arrived at Lombard to discover that the Jawbone was snowbound. This resulted in a three week delay. We stayed at Billy Kee's hotel there and eventually got a job with the railroad shoveling snow.

"We left Lombard at 8:00 in the morning and after almost four hours we had gone five miles. It was time to eat lunch and no provisions were made for eating on the train so Mr. Rantool, the manager of the Jawbone made arrangements for lunch at the Piegon Ranch another mile up the creek. We got as far as Dorsey before dark and after shoveling until midnight we got to Summit. We were hungry and exhausted from all of that work. At 4:00 a.m. the engineer awakened Mr. Rantool and advised him that the wind was blowing the track shut again and that we'd better get going. Mr. Rantool declined and went back to sleep saying that the wind was a chinook. We had nothing but trouble from there on. The snow plow on the train was attached to a flat bed car and we hadn't gone even a mile when it rode a drift over the rails. It took hours to right the plow and get it back on the tracks. The train backed into town.

"Mr. Black and I got disgusted then, deciding to ride horses to our homestead. We followed the tracks then on horseback all of the way to the Gap between the Snowies and Belt mountain ranges.

"That ride became a nightmare because after we had ridden about five miles through a raging blizzard, night time overtook us. We hadn't seen another horse or human since we left the train and we were wondering where we could spend the night. The way the snow was falling we knew that the railroad tracks would soon be covered. I then noticed horses tracks and the runners of a sleigh and we followed that to a sheep ranch. They were losing sheep by the hundreds because they were short on feed. The next day we made it our destination the next day after passing through the Lou Sigafoos place north of Garneill where we had to pick our way over the bodies of hundreds of dead cattle.

"I wired my wife to come on the next train, figuring that the railroad would be open again but it wasn't. She too, spent almost three weeks at Lombard waiting for the tracks to get shoveled out. The depot agent at Moore wasn't very busy because a train had not been to Moore in almost two months. Nevertheless, I managed to talk to my wife at Lombard and make arrangements for her to go on to Great Falls where she could catch the stage from there to Moore. It was a happy re-union despite the fact that it took almost fifty hours to get there from Great Falls. She had only one bottle of milk for the baby and no way to heat it but somehow everyone survived.

"I heard that a train was finally going to arrive on February 12th. It was expected in Moore at 3:00 in the afternoon. Mr. Rantool had assessed a $40.00 charge against each of our cars as a feed bill for our livestock. We never did pay it figuring that they had inconvenienced us enough without added charges.

"We stayed with friends that we had made until April 12th when we moved into a cabin owned by Scott Campbell. We stayed there until our shack was finished enough so that we could move into it.

"Our new neighbors were the finest people I've ever met. They all pitched in and helped us unload the stock when that train finally arrived. I had no place to keep them and nothing to feed them so one of the neighbors volunteered to take care of them until we could handle the. When I asked what I owed him he said that it was a neighborly act done out of neighborliness not for money.

"Then in 1918, my wife, who was a real helpmate caught the flu and died. Things were never the same after that.

"Those early homesteaders were a tough lot in order to survive the many hardships of settling a new land. And many of them had several tough years in a row. And surely, homestead women earned themselves a very special place in heaven."

Henry O'Donnell, fireman, under cab of Montana Railroad No. 5. A 4-6-0. Others in this 1905 photo not identified.

Warren McGee collection

CHAPTER VII

RUMORS

In addition to constant ridicule by the state's newspapers, rumors circulated regarding the future of the Montana Railroad. Harlow not only didn't counter these rumors, but in fact gave reason to believe that he did have additional plans for expansion. A strong suspicion nourished the notion that he planned to return to the financial well and find the resources for building the Montana east of Lewistown through the rest of central Montana and into North Dakota. He never denied that what Hill had done north of the Missouri River in Montana, he could do south of the river, opening up a vast agricultural area. Building a third railroad link to the Twin Cities of St. Paul and Minneapolis didn't seem a farfetched idea after what he'd already accomplished. Another rumor persisted in surfacing that the Chicago, Milwaukee, and St. Paul Railroad planned to expand west through Montana as the third transcontinental line. This deal actually materialized in 1906 when that railroad decided upon a western expansion. The Montana Railroad became important to their plans for that extension.

The original idea centered around leasing the Montana's trackage and connecting to it from both the east at Harlowton and the west at Lombard. Ultimately, when the time was right a purchase option could be exercised that would acquire the entire 157 mile Montana Railroad.

With this arrangement, Harlow now had a deal in which a troublesome stretch of trackage would ge maintained by a more financially able railroad. He also had the onus of satisfying a first mortgage committment to James Hill of the Great Northern and his bonds with the Northern Pacific. It took two years to hammer out these details, but in 1908, the Milwaukee finally purchased the entire Montana Railroad.

The Smith River searched northerly toward Ulm and its confluence with the Missouri. The Shields River flowed south to join the Yellowstone River and Sixteen Mile Creek tumbled out of the Crazy Mountains to its rendezvous with the Missouri at Lombard. The valley at Ringling was indeed a watershed. Montana's major asset, water, was available in abundance and attracting gullible pioneers was simple.

The Milwaukee examined its newly acquired geography, then set upon a program of extolling, exuberance, extravagance, exaggeration, and what ultimately appeared to be extortion. The advertising programs were international in scope and each burgeoning community erected billboards along the sidetrack adjacent to the depot touting the potential of the surrounding terrain. The homestead movement exploded with the Milwaukee Railroad the primary beneficiary. They brought the settlers and their goods to the homestead with the promise of carrying the produce of the good land to eager and hungry markets to the east.

Milwaukee Railroad plans for expansion called for extending branch lines out of Lewistown in the remaining three directions, east to Winnett, west to Great Falls, and north to Roy, all prime homestead country. The potential of this promotion was staggering and little farm towns blossomed on the prairies, following on the heels of the construction. An entirely new economy swept over the opened country based upon farming quarter section and half section tracts.

A section house was built each fifteen mile interval, where the section foreman and his family lived while maintenance of right-of-way occupied his long working hours. He was often the first citizen of what became a town built around the sidetrack that had been built there. Hundreds of children were born in section houses as women joined their husbands in settling the open country. This population explosion took place throughout the high plains of Montana, with boomlets occuring between Roundup and Forsyth, Miles City and Marmarth, North Dakota, as well as what had been the Jawbone country.

The land boom was of such proportions that it merited the Milwaukee's serious attention and enormous investment. Hundreds of tiny farm towns were built on the plains and in the mountains of Montana. Usually fifteen miles separated them, but they were very much alike. All of them featured stock-loading pens, grain elevators, mercantile stores, blacksmith shop, hotel, bar, often a bank, a church or two, and a school created a prairie skyline. Where labor intensive activities took place, multiples of bars, brothels, cafes, and hotels were built surrounding the railroad yards. Respectable women were rare at first, outnumbered by men by ratios of five and ten to one. Ladies of the night became a part of the communities' affairs. Their business was usually managed by a respected madame.

Many of these villages became ethnic enclaves in their own right. Brothers joined other members of their father's families from Minnesota, Indiana, Illinois, Wisconsin, Scandinavia, and Germany to establish themselves in a new town. Norwegians outnumbered all others by far. It wasn't unusual to discover that each citizen was related to another in the new town. Usually within a year, married women joined their husbands on the farms or in the towns. More sturdy looking banks, schools, and churches added to the appearance of the homestead town.

The highly successful promotional and advertising program of the Milwaukee Railroad featured a plow turning virgin sod with dollar bills surrounding the blade of the plow. Every Milwaukee office between Chicago and St. Paul pictured the abundance of land and its deep, rich soil. The state's moderate climate was boasted along with cheap and plentiful land. The railroad acquired up to two hundred forty acres of land along its sidetracks that it subdivided and sold to the town's future Main Street merchants. The advertising program was international in scope, tugging at land starved Europeans for a response. There was little that remained to the imagination for development and exploitation.

The major portion of the land boom took place between 1910 and 1915. World War I accelerated the need for farming and crops. with the world's need to be fed and prices at historic highs. While there were some who couldn't tolerate the isolation or the physical demands of farming and failed to prove up their homestead, most did. With easy credit and high demand, the railroad's promises appeared fulfilled. But the end of the war marked the immediate collapse of the noble experiment and the beginning of the end.

At that time, a virulent influenza epidemic swept across the entire nation, filling hospitals and eventually closing schools, which in turn, were promptly converted to hospitals. Many of the youngest and the oldest died of pneumonia. Someone in nearly every family was critically ill. The following three years were ones of extreme drought conditions. A credit crisis forced the closure of two-thirds of the small town banks in these small Montana towns. Some counties dropped from seven banks to none between 1921 and 1923. Doors and windows were boarded along Main Street and abandoned farms were scattered across the searing prairie.

There were banks too broke to foreclose and farmers and ranchers too poor to afford the expense of moving. Neither could liquidate their liberty bonds at the twenty-five percent discount that was offered. The farm towns that had sprung up in the wake of the Jawbone named Buffalo and Straw were soon to slide into limbo and those that were strictly railroad towns, named Bruno and Sixteen, were soon to collapse altogether. The economy of this section of Montana wasn't only depressed, it was demolished.

CHAPTER VIII

Closing the Sale

The ink had no more than dried on the lease-purchase agreement between the Chicago, Milwaukee, St. Paul and Puget Sound Railroad and the Montana Railroad when reconstruction commenced. There was little doubt in the minds of either party to the transaction that a purchase was imminent. But James Hill the empire builder held the trump card, the first mortgage on the Montana Railroad. At the first hint of default, he was in position to acquire all of the real estate with little effort or expense.

Three years later, in 1909, while he was on an ocean liner headed for Europe, Hill's mortgage was paid off. A satisfaction was recorded and possession of all of the Montana's assets was delivered to the Milwaukee. Hill was out of his office in St. Paul and out of the country when his aides were delivered the money paying off the mortgage.

Simultaneously, the bonds with the Northern Pacific were brought current and Harlow at last had the huge burden of enormous debt lifted from his shoulders.

But even during that three-year period of leasehold interest, the Milwaukee moved quickly to bring significant improvements to their trackage. The heavier traffic and trains mandated a better base than what

was originally built by Lombard and Harlow.

They tore up the sections where there was little if any ballast, laying a solid foundation of pit run gravel. The Milwaukee's theory was that pit run material was less damaging to the ties than crushed rock. This practice continued throughout the tenure of the Milwaukee in Montana. They straightened curves, reduced grades, and undertook the largest project of all, that of moving the roadbed above the creek bottom throughout Sixteen Mile Canyon. This was as large a task as the original building. Dorsey and New Dorsey were bypassed by the new routing from Summit to Leader.

This lifting of the grade involved the building of five tunnels through the mountainsides of the canyon.

Tunnel number one on the Milwaukee was located at Tomah, Wisconsin. Therefore, the numbering from east to west through the canyon commenced with tunnel number two.

A chart, showing the five tunnels, follows:

Tunnel	Location	Length	Date of construction
2	Fanalulu	378 '	April to September 1907
3	1.4 miles west of Canyon	157 '	April to August 1907
4	1.7 miles east of Canyon	312 '	April to June 1908
5	1.2 miles east of Josephine	315 '	June 07 to July 08
6	1.9 miles east of Deer Park	476 '	April 07 to June 08

Leader, Montana, later renamed Ringling, was destined to become the queen city of the Smith River valley. It was one and a half miles from Dorsey on a one percent grade from west to east. During those days of steam power, water tanks and coal tipples were spotted at Bruno, Fanalulu, and Lennep as well as Leader. The size of the reconstruction project assured these little villages a brief glimpse of prosperity, hosting hotels, saloons, a livery, and a brothel or two along the town's main street. But Dorsey was destined to be passed by the new roadbed and it and its twin city, New Dorsey, were victims of the Milwaukee's progress.

Following the reconstruction, the Milwaukee made a profitable and dependable railroad out of what had been the Montana Railroad. Branch lines were built into Great Falls in 1914, a huge depot was built along the Missouri River in that city, and the massive yards hinted that the Milwaukee was preparing to compete with Jim Hill's Great Northern. Another branch was built to Winnett in 1917, just a year ahead of the Great Northern's plans, hence the newly settled plains of eastern Fergus County and the Cat Creek Oil Field were captured by the aggressive newcomer, the Milwaukee Railroad.

The most profound announcement was yet to originate at the Chicago headquarters of the Milwaukee. During the construction of the line through the Cascade Mountains of Washington, sufficient right-of-way was purchased to facilitate the use of electric power. It was the Milwaukee's plan to electrify throughout the mountains of the West. Their original concept called for them to harness the many streams in the mountains and generate their own electricity. The announcement was made in 1915 that the Milwaukee would electrify from Harlowton west to Avery, Idaho, across St. Paul Pass from Saltese, Montana. The second contract to be let was the one that brought electricity to the railroad between Harlowton and Lombard, the original routing of the Montana Railroad. It was a momentous occasion that was celebrated along the line and cursed by the railroad's competitors.

The cost of the electrification of the Milwaukee Railroad system was estimated to be $12,000,000 in construction and $3,000,000 in equipment. General Electric was awarded the contract for locomotives and power stations through the Rocky Mountains, and then the Cascades in Washington were eventually brought under wire in

1920. The Idaho division between Avery, Idaho, and Othello, Washington, was never electrified for a number of reasons. The passenger tracks ran north to Spokane and the freight trackage went straight west from St. Maries through Malden to Othello. This section became known as the "gap" because steam and then diesel remained the primary power source.

Montana benefitted from the introduction of electrically powered locomotives. There was no smoke, soot, or noise abatements required. The electrics earned the reputation of thriving on the cold weather and in head to head competitions consistently outpulled the more cantankerous steam engines. The Milwaukee was the first railroad to light their coaches with electricity early in the century and the management was satisified with the performance of electric motors in interurban and commuter services between Chicago and Milwaukee.

General Electric delivered the first of the box cab electrics in 1915, ten months after signing the contract for their construction. The last of thirty motors was delivered in 1917.

The catenary was built between Harlowton and Three Forks, Montana, as the second contract in 1915. The first section built was between Three Forks and Deer Lodge, traveling through Butte, Montana's most populous city at the time. This connection allowed the Milwaukee to witness the use of electricity in the operation of the Butte, Anaconda, and Pacific Railroad, a short line that served the Anaconda Company. It was there that the decision to buy power from the Montana Power Company was reached. No hydroelectric plants were built in Montana. The substations were subsequently built at Two Dot and Loweth, formerly known as Summit along the Montana Railroad between Harlowton and Lombard. Loweth was the name of the electrical engineer who designed the Milwaukee grid system.

The electrification sounded the death knell for Lombard and several smaller towns. There was no need for coal and water supply stations, so Lombard declined and Bruno was dissolved in a short period of time.

Sixteen Mile Canyon was renamed "Montana Canyon" as a tribute to the original railroad, and all of the Milwaukee literature featured that name. Yet it quickly reverted to Sixteen Mile Canyon as the Milwaukee began to lose its influence upon maps and advertising.

The canyon was the scenic wonder of the new railroad, with pristine Sixteen Mile Creek the centerpiece of its beauty. Maintenance of right-of-way employees stationed at Sixteen, Josephine, and Deer Park were issued snake bite kits by the railroad company and they frequently hung snake skins on the barbed wire fences to further charm the passengers on the Olympian and the Columbian passenger trains. The Milwaukee attached an open air car at Ringling to accommodate the picture-taking passengers as the two crack passenger trains made their way west to Lombard where the open air car was disconnected and waited for the next eastbound passenger train.

Riding the luxurious accommodations of the Milwaukee was a far cry from the primitive coaches and mixed trains of the Jawbone. The coaches and Pullmans were heated, lighted, and then air conditioned in the thirties. Transcontinental passenger service featured dining car service and an observation car that was the ultimate in accommodations. The platform at the rear of the train provided space for the travelers who were seeking fresh air. The quiet electric motors traveled up or down grade at the same steady speed. Drifting snow and frigid temperatures didn't hamper their operation and they appeared to thrive on adverse weather conditions - the same climate that plagued the performance of the Montana Railroad.

Eventually the railroad owned eighty-four of the General Electric box cabs, adding ten General Electric steeple cab units as switch engines, five of which were bipolar units. The Milwaukee was loyal to General Electric in that only ten Baldwin Westinghouse motors were ever put into

The Milwaukee called it "Montana Canyon" on their timetable, "Sixteen Mile Canyon" in their publicity. Note parallel trackage, 1935.   Gordon Irion collection

Milwaukee publicity photo, showing both Milwaukee and Montana Railroad trackage, 1935.
                                                                Gordon Irion collection

service. Finally, twelve General Electric articulates were purchased immediately after World War II when the deal to sell them to the Soviet Union fell through. These were called "Little Joes" by the railroad employees, named for Joseph Stalin. The electrics owed the Milwaukee nothing when the electric system was abandoned in 1973, just in time for expensive diesel fuel.

Despite its many improvements the Milwaukee Railroad in Montana was not without its problems. There were none more serious than the earthquake on June 28, 1925. The epicenter of the quake focused upon Three Forks and Manhattan, but the damage was widespread in White Sulphur Springs as well. It was felt in a wide area, bringing people out of their homes and businesses throughout Montana.

The courthouse and school were substantially destroyed in White Sulphur Springs, several buildings in Three Forks and Manhatten were leveled by the quivering

earth and the following aftershocks. Damage was estimated to be in the hundreds of thousands of dollars, ranging from cracks in the plaster of the capitol building at Helena to the crumbling of several brick buildings in the towns along the front range of the Rockies. Newspaper accounts were often in conflict because all telegraph services were disrupted in the affected areas.

An avalanche followed the earthquake at Lombard, sliding tons of the mountainside into the Missouri River, blocking the trackage of the Northern Pacific there. But the damage to the Milwaukee in the canyon was added to the financial railroad operating in a depressed economy. The tunnel at Deer Park was closed, an avalanche there dammed Sixteen Mile Creek, and continuing aftershocks frustrated the first attempts at keeping the lines open.

The sleepy village of Deer Park, home to a section foreman, was isolated from the rest of the world while the rising waters of

David Shearer, wife, and family camped at the construction camp at Sixteen, Montana, in 1907.

the creek swirled about it. Sixteen Mile Creek was also dammed by the force of the earthquake. Torrential rains followed the 6:30 p.m. shaker, creating even more problems for the shorthanded crews. It was soon apparent to all that there was no way to temporarily fix what nature had destroyed. The stream became a roaring torrent filling the avalanche created dam with sixty feet of water. The bridges and tracks were under water within hours after the first shocks.

When daybreak revealed the damage, tons of rock had slid into the canyon bottom. The rains unloosened fragile soil conditions and continued to tumble into what had been a creek but now a growing body of water. There was little that remained of the original trackage.

The Milwaukee's first estimates of damage totaled a million dollars. This was soon revised to total a million, five hundred thousand dollars.

Twenty miles of the canyon trackage were destroyed, and while fifteen hundred men went to work repairing it, the Olympian and the Columbian were rerouted over Northern Pacific tracks from Miles City to Sappington. Freight trains were detoured over the Great Northern. What was originally thought to be a one week job became one that consumed the entire summer of 1925.

The resulting lake created its own kind of problem. Deep sea divers were brought into the task from Seattle. Their assignment was to reopen the channel along the creek bed, draining the impounded water. Weekly newspapers from the affected communities of White Sulphur Spings, Three Forks, and Manhattan reported that workmen of every nationality were soon dispatched to the scene. Lombard served as headquarters for the damage repair task. The Northern Pacific had its own landslide to

Rebuilding the main line after purchase by the Milwaukee Railroad. This was the box canyon. David Shearer on horse, 1907.
Warren McGee collection

repair at that site.

A shoe fly was built around the mountain at the Deer Park tunnel. This was temporary trackage alongside the mountain. The tunnel had suffered enormous damage and the shoe fly was a temporary passage while tunnel repairs were made.

The embattled railroad, already beset by financial problems, pulled the throttle on the repair work. The tons of rock and earth that had collapsed into the creek were removed and hauled away, the rails were relaid, bridges were rebuilt, and the tunnel at Deer Park was essentially reexcavated. The telegraph system that paralleled the Milwaukee was restrung as was the electrification system.

The damage estimates grew as time passed during the summer. The theater, school, bank building, and telephone exchange were all ultimately condemned and demolished in the interest of safety in Manhattan. Three Forks witnessed the destruction of its school, the Methodist church, and both of its banks, the American National and the Labor National banks.

A massive crack appeared between the two towns that ranged from two to five inches wide with a depth of up to five feet. There was no such a thing as a Richter scale at the time, but a professor of geology at the University of Montana, Dr. C. D. Clapp, explained the phenomena with stories that were carried by all of the state's newspapers. "It was a slippage of the earth, a common thing along the Rocky Mountain front."

A total of forty-one shocks were felt during and following the major event on Saturday, June 28th, 1925. The area has long since been recognized as one of growing mountains and occasional severe shocks.

It was considered a miracle that no one was killed in the disaster that struck on that warm summer evening. The mines at Butte and Jardine were shaken but did not collapse. Yellowstone and Glacier national parks were rattled by the earthquake with some avalanche activity following it. But the earth's shaking had more lasting calamitous results on the Milwaukee Railroad than it

Don Baker

Sixteen Mile Canyon, Creek and tunnel

had on anything else in the earthquake's area of influence. For the Milwaukee, it hastened the day of financial calamity.

Because of the difficult times that the railroad encountered during its last fifty years, the cost of replacing the catenary system was overwhelming. The fir poles were untreated, resulting in wood rot. They were propped with short stubs, but even those began to erode, and all in all the condition of the electric lines was poor, requiring more cash to renovate them than the railroad could afford or justify at the time.

The electric dream perished about the same time that passenger service became unprofitable.

But the character of the entire Jaw-bone Railroad had changed within twenty years after the Milwaukee bought it. Its light weight rail was replaced with heavy duty steel. The shallow and nonexistent ballast was rebuilt and curves were eliminated while grades were reduced with the use of tunnels. The huffing and puffing underpowered steam engines were replaced with humming electric motors. The railroad became a model of efficiency and cost effectiveness. At times, the electric motors were the only ones in the Rocky Mountain Division that were not frozen to a dead stop. What had been a laughingstock among railroad circles became the envy of the Rocky Mountain West. But the lingering depression that followed World War I finally drove even the Milwaukee into

Don Baker

The Milwaukee's Eagle Nest Tunnel in Sixteen Mile Canyon, 1985.

bankruptcy in 1925, along with the area that it served with such initial enthusiasm.

When the final bankruptcy came to pass in 1980, the railroad wasn't even a skeleton of its former self. Deferred maintenance of both equipment and real estate had pounded the final nail in its coffin. It was abandoned west of Miles City, never to see another silk train, fast freight, crack passenger outfit, or even an attempt to resurrect the greatness of its past. Soon, all physical evidence of a railroad had vanished from Miles City through Vananda, Ingomar, Roundup, Harlowton, Ringling, and beautiful Sixteen Mile Canyon.

Don Baker   **Eagle Nest Tunnel near Sixteen.**

Don Baker   **Milwaukee Tunnel in Sixteen Mile Canyon, 1985**
Don Baker   **The Milwaukee's Josephine Tunnel in Sixteen Mile Canyon, 1985**

Milwaukee trestle and tunnel in Sixteen Mile Canyon, 1985.   Don Baker

Don Baker

Sixteen Mile Creek through Sixteen Mile (or Montana) Canyon.
Montana Railroad grade on the right, Milwaukee on the left, 1985.

Honest John's Saloon, Ringling

A panoramic view of Ringling, Montana in 1916, taken from atop a boxcar and shown here split into two pictures.

Don Baker   **Ringling**

St. John's Catholic Church at Ringling, 1985.   **Don Baker**

Don Baker   **Sixteen, Montana, 1985.**

A busy day at Harlowton depot, 1941.

Phil and Lee Rostad collection

Ron and Cheryl Schrader collection

A Milwaukee Railroad local, 1937.

Harlowton yards before electrification, 1910.

Gordon Irion

Ed Burroughs

"Little Joe" under wire at Harlowton, 1956.

Milwaukee's four electrics at Harlowton, 1951

Gordon Irion

The shoe fly built following the 1925 earthquake. The tunnel at Deer Park collapsed, requiring that it be rebored.

The Milwaukee Railroad building the Missouri River bridge at Lombard, 1907.   Warren McGee collection

Warren McGee collection   Montana Railroad passenger train departing Lombard for Harlowton

Lombard during the construction of the Missouri River Bridge, 1907.

Warren McGee collection

Lombard shops and wye, 1907. New Milwaukee tracks bridge Sixteen Mile Creek and Montana Railroad mainline to NP interchange.

Warren McGee collection

Wareen McGee collection

Lombard, Montana, 1907.

CHAPTER IX

REMINISCING

Tom LeFever engineered on the Jawbone and then the Milwaukee until he retired. His memoirs are captured in handwritten notes. He recalls:

"I was part of the crew that took the Leadborough branch down in 1904. There had been very little traffic on it for years and as a result the tracks were over-run with grass and weeds and the bridge pilings looked very rotten.

"There was a question about whether or not it would hold the work train. The trestle was quite long so the bridge crew wanted me, the engineer to walk across it and then the fireman would start the engine across the bridge. I would then catch it and stop it after it got across unless the bridge collapsed, which it didn't do.

"Then we started up a grade and then down one about a mile where the rails were covered with timothy grass. It was so slick that even with the brakes set, the train wouldn't stop. In fact, it turned into a sled. It finally did stop just one rail length from the Leadborough depot.

"There had been many snow sheds built along the tracks between Leadborough and the trestle over Warm Springs Creek. The crew cut the depot in half, loaded the halves on a flat car and eventually they became the depots at Straw and Two Dot.

"The grade was so stout and the grass had made the rails so slippery that the work crew was cutting grass and sprinkling the rails with sand all of the way to Summit. It was a much longer job than what anyone had estimated it would be because of these conditions.

"I originally went to work for the railroad at Summit because my dad worked there for them. I had been born on Duck Creek, a few miles north of Canton, fourteen miles north of Townsend on April 1, 1887. My parents lived in a cabin with a dirt floor. Dad and mother had moved from Virginia, near Washington, D.C. in 1882. He owned and operated a saw mill until 1902 when he went to work as a section foreman at Summit for the old Jawbone Railroad.

"Dad was paid with post dated checks in those days and they were given board and room. If an employee stayed thirty days, he was given clothing, a completely new outfit to wear.

"Mr. Billy Kee at Lombard cashed all of the Jawbone checks and eventually they were all as good as gold.

"When I first went to work for them, the railroad was mostly owned by Mr. Harlow, Mr. Lombard, and Mrs. Rantool, the widow of the first superintendent of the railroad. I went to work for $1.25 a day, ten hours a day. I worked on the section crew for two years when I went to work watching engines. At the time, there were two engines between Summit and Lewistown and one between Summit and Lombard. My job consisted of cooling the engines down when they layed over at Summit. I broke up the fire and put them in the house to cool off. And then I started them up again early in the morning. They left for Lewistown at about noon.

"One morning I couldn't get a fire started in the engine because the netting in the stack was fouled. The fire just smouldered in the pit and went out. Ordinarily, I would just beat the shovel on the stack and free the soot and goo out of the netting but that wouldn't work this morning. So, I filled a condensed milk can with gasoline and tossed it into the fire pit figuring that that would blow it open. It did. And it blew the fire door open throwing me against the coal gate. I wiped the ashes and dust off of my face and started the fire going real well. The netting had blown out of the stack and looked like a mushroom. The superintendent never did know that I was responsible for turning his spark arrestor inside out and that locomotive was throwing sparks all over or I would have been fired.

"I also kept the steam up when the crew and passengers were in the cafe eating lunch. I once shoveled a box of dynamite into the fire box. It had been left in the coal at the mine and when I saw what I had done I ran for the tall timber. But all it did was burn. It never did explode, thank God.

"The superintendent always came with the train on the first day of the month to give the men their pay checks. On this particular day, the fireman was slow eating and everyone was ready to return to Lombard except him. The superintendent had one of his grouches on and hired me on the spot to fire the engine on the return trip. That's how I got started on the engine crew for the Jawbone.

"My mother ran the eating house at

G.R. Haines

Milwaukee 23/8 arriving in Great Falls during the winter of 1929.

Summit and would feed up to a hundred twenty people a day traveling between Lewistown and Lombard. The only day that trains didn't run was Sunday.

"I worked for the Northern Pacific for a little while until I went back to the Jawbone in 1906. W. McKenna, Dan Burlingame and I worked out of Lewistown hauling material to the Milwaukee while it was under construction between Melstone and Harlowton. Then we worked the Shooflies between Lombard and Harlowton. While we did that we had a terrible time with a bull that always challenged our train. He always picked a steep part of the track to snort up the middle of the rails and slow us to five or six miles an hour. So we had an awful time getting up the grade trying to nudge him along near Deer Park. Finally, McKenna met Mr. Bull on the down grade and that finsihed the bull.

"It often took us two days to make the trip because we always had problems. There was no water in the tanks or another train was in our way. There was no end to the number of reasons why the Jawbone would be delayed.

"The winters where the Jawbone went were real difficult. I worked on the section in 1903 when entire trains were buried in snow for months on end. The train from Lewistown to Harlowton got stuck in the snow for two months starting the 21st of February. And then the train to Lombard got stuck two miles east of Summit on the 22nd, the day after. There were twenty-four passengers on board who were taken by bob sled to White Sulphur Springs after two days of living on what was on board. A whole beef and three hogs were being transported from Kendall to Dorsey. They prepared the food in the fire pit of the engine. The train finally got shovelled out on April 6th.

"My parents lived at Summit and dad kept three hogs in the roundhouse then that he intended to butcher later on. Every, night, wolves came to the building and tried to break in and kill the hogs. Finally, dad brought the dog into the house to secure the doors against the wolves. Even at that, they came right up to house door and clawed and scratched trying to get at the dog.

"We broke up so many engines that the Northern Pacific wouldn't let us use anymore of theirs. George Murray went to Chicago to pick out an engine that they weren't using. If old number five was the best of the bunch, like George said it was, I'd sure hate to have seen the others. It took about a week to fix it up at Lombard so it would run and then when it was taken out to run up to the stuck passenger train it collided with a box car that had been spotted on the main line by the Butler ranch. That smashed up the engine good again so it was towed back to Lombard for another week. After that the fire pan began to leak. By then, the N.P. let us have another engine but insisted that they furnish the cab crew. I guess they didn't really trust us with their equipment after that winter. Their crew got as far as Dorsey and then they gave up to the snow drifts leaving the engine there. A Jawbone crew took that engine then and hooked it to a flat car that had been loaded with rail to prevent it from breaking in halves. The work crew installed a plow that had been broken off of one of the first engines to the flat car. They would back up a mile or two and take a running start at the snow banks, some of which were almost fifty feet high and one was eleven miles long. The flat car filled with snow then and when they would back it off, the work crews would shovel snow from the flat car. During that first night, the wind came up again and completely filled the cuts. The plow ended up more than three miles from the engine. Mr. Rantool, the general manager, ordered that the plow be kept at Dorsey. It took us three days to shovel our way to the plow and another three days to plow our way to Summit. Some of the banks of snow were so high that men took turns sliding down the banks on scoop shovels. George Murray, one of the engineers burned his butt taking one of those rides and couldn't sit down for a week.

'We ran into five horses that had sought shelter in one of the cuts. One of the horses had slipped through the ties on a bridge and when the engine hit him the plow broke off of the engine. It had no lights because they had all been broken by ice and snow. Some of the crews who stuck those trains walked up to fifteen miles to the town of Sixteen or rode hand cars through the canyon to Lombard, leaving the train out on the tracks. I don't know how many trains were scattered along the Jawbone that winter altogether. Three barrels of whiskey bound for Harlowton, Ubet and Lewistown were empty when the seven car train was finally freed. The whiskey barrels looked like a porcupine where crews had driven ten penny nails into them and then filled a pitcher with whiskey. Some of the crews hadn't had a change of clothing or a bath in two months when they could finally get out of the snow.

"Most of those winters were called 'Dakotas' because they were so fierce. The temperatures would often go down to forty or fifty below zero and the wind would blow at sixty miles an hour for three or four days. Considering the few people who lived out in the country between Lewistown and Harlowton then, it was amazing how many died in the storms each winter.

"A Jawbone crew got as far as three miles west of Judith Gap with a light engine that they were bringing to Lombard for repair when they got stalled. They finally ended up camping out in the fire box. They crawled out in three days, digging a passageway between the cab of the engine and the tender. The snow had drifted over the entire train. They had eaten a few crackers and four cans of sardines. They killed a jack rabbit and cooked it in the engine without salt or bread or anything else. The next day they walked three miles to a ranch house. They were so covered with soot that the ranch woman slammed the door in their faces. They were sick in bed then for several days before a railroad crew came looking for them. They had found the engine but had no idea where the crew was. Another passenger train took thirty days to go thirty miles.

"Another train spent four days at a siding at Oka completely bogged down by a four day storm. The blowing snow was so bad that there were times when they couldn't see the section house, only thirty feet away. A train came from Harlowton to pick up passengers and a bobsled came from Lewistown to take those passengers back to Lewistown. Included among them were a bride and groom named Heidenreich.

"There were three school teachers who froze to death near the Gap when they discovered that their matches were wet and they couldn't start a fire in their homestead shack. And a man froze to death just a mile or so out of town. Those were hard winters.

"During the fall of 1907 I was given the job of keeping snow plowed off of the tracks between Harlowton and Lewistown. My engine was a high wheeled outfit that was capable of speeds up to eighty miles an hours. Sometimes we made three round trips per day clearing the way for the two passenger trains and one freight per day.

"The Great Northern ran through Judith Gap too with a passenger service between Billings and Great Falls. That winter of 1907 they had a wreck between Judith Gap and Nihill when the superintendent and the dispatcher at the Gap sent a passenger train ten minutes after the freight. About five miles out of town, the freight stalled in a snow drift. The entire crew tried to dig it out while the brakeman walked back to set flares and warn the passenger train's crew. None of the passenger engine crew saw him, his flares nor his torpedoes because of the blowing snow. As a result, the passenger ran into the rear of the freight. The passenger's fireman was building a fire in the fire box when they hit and he flew head first into the fire box. The engineer grabbed him as quickly as he could by the ankles and pulled him out. But the fireman was fully cooked with his hand firmly grasped to the handle of his coal shovel. The jolt of the collision freed the freight's locomotive from the drifted snow and the train rolled without engine crew for ten or twelve more miles until it hit another snow drift.

"We'd buck against the snow drift until the wheels just spun on the engine.

Then we'd back up for a mile or so, building more fire and steam in the boiler. We'd get going as fast as we could then, sometimes hitting the snow drift at seventy or eighty miles an hour. It's just a wonder that we didn't jump the tracks or upend the engine. My fireman, Gannon and I were just twenty years old and neither one of us knew what fear was all about. Sometimes when we returned to Harlowton, we saw the chunks of dirt mixed with snow and ice that we had plowed off of the tracks on the way up. We took a superintendent and forty men in a coach with us to clear the right of way. The superintendent thought that if we got stuck the forty men could dig us out. The reason that this was so important was that there was a passenger train stuck between Moore and Lewistown and our job was to break them loose. After bucking snow drifts and filled cuts for twenty miles all of their cups of coffee had spilled all over the floor of the coach. The superintendent told me, 'I've never been so scared in my life. In fact, I've wet my pants, you see.'

"Nevertheless, when we got to Lewistown he bought my fireman and me a drink and dinner.

"There were only two firemen who were comfortable with me. Otto Heines and Homer Gannon. We ran engines for more than fifty years, 3,000,000 miles and thousands of passengers without ever hurting anyone.

"Another veteran engineer, George Murray had a few experiences with cats that remained with him the rest of his life. He pumped a hand car from Lombard to Maudlow to go to a dance there. He heard a noise behind him when he came out of a tunnel at Deer Park so he looked behind and lo and behold, there was a mountain lion running along behind him. Those hand cars were propelled by pumping with the feet and pushing with the arms. He went as fast as he could go, stopping at the side track in Maudlow, running as hard as he could to the hotel where the dance was. He was so out of breath that he laid down on a bed and rested for an hour or so.

"He was forever afraid of the dark after that incident and it seems that every scary thing that happened to him on the railroad happened after the sun had set. We were once bringing an engine from Lewistown to Lombard for repair when we stopped at Summit to have supper with my parents. While there my sister took five cats in a sack to the tender for me to deliver to the water tank at Groveland where some friends of hers were expecting them and would pick them up after I left them. As we passed through Deer Park, a cat screamed out and George's hair stood straight up on end. His eyes looked like tea cups, he was so scared. Then the next night, I put the sack full of cats out at the water tank. While I was connecting the hose to the tank on the tender, George walked around the engine oiling it. His torch caught the eyes of several of the cats and he about jumped out of his skin. He leaped into the cab, pulled the throttle and away we went with the hose still connected. We had all sort of adventures, running into livestock and game on the trackage. And there were many times when we lost our brakes on those one to four percent grades.

"Through the years I had many brushes with death when the engine went one way on the switch and the tender and cars went down the main line. Many crewmen jumped off of the train when it derailed and that was sure death. During the dark of night there was no way of telling if you jumped when the train was on a bridge or a narrow cut where you'd just roll under the wheels.

"The curves were so tight in Sixteen Mile Canyon that there were several train wrecks because there was so little visibility. And often, the conductor or brakeman failed to set out flags to slow down following trains.

"Shortly after the Milwaukee took over, the reconstruction of the grades over Summit was started and the tracks were elevated above the stream bed in the canyon. It took two years to rebuild but it was a much safer railroad after that was done."

CHAPTER X

The Spartan Railroad

Another Helena attorney, Lew Penwell, envisioned a railroad serving the Smith River valley, reaching White Sulphur Springs, and realizing that community's hopes of twenty years.

Penwell was called the "man who believed in Montana" by *Leslie's Illustrated Weekly Newspaper*. His accomplishments beginning in 1910 prove that. Penwell organized several corporations for the express purpose of acquiring land, subdividing it into smaller farming units, and selling it to newly arrived settlers at a tidy profit. His first venture was the Smith River country.

At one time he owned more than twenty-five ranching companies that consisted of more than 4,000,000 acres of land. The Smith River coup, though, was his most unusual and daring accomplishment. He raised $50,000 for the express purpose of taking options on all the land between Leader and White Sulphur Springs where this new railroad would run. His confidence and efforts were applauded by the White Sulphur Springs newspapers, the *Rocky Mountain Husbandman* and the Meagher Country *Republican*, both of whom believed that White Sulphur Springs would boom as a tourist center when it was served by a railroad.

Penwell was raised on a ranch in Gallatin County and eventually went to Columbia University where he studied to become a lawyer. While there he met John Ringling, who was to become a notable circus magnate. Penwell soon discovered after graduation that few lawyers did very well in their practice and, like Harlow, he began to dabble in real estate. He lost his one attempt to become a county attorney and he wasn't interested in being an assistant to anyone. Therefore, he decided to terminate his legal career and concentrate on land development and its promotion.

He persuaded Ringling to join him in this railroad promotion and eventually sold the Chicago, Milwuakee, St. Paul and Puget Sound heirarchy a fifty-one percent equity in the line that would join them at Leader, soon to be renamed Ringling in honor of its most distinguished citizen.

The railroad was to run a distance of twenty-three miles, zigging and zagging over a distance of eighteen miles as the many birds flew. It was christened the White Sulphur Springs and Yellowstone Park Railroad, an ambitious name for a short line, but the original plans called for it to be a park to park railroad, headquartered in White

Sulphur Springs, soon to realize its potential as a tourist mecca.

The Montana Daily Record reported that $3,000,000 would be spent in developing the Smith River Valley and the grand hotel planned for White Sulphur Springs.

These pronouncements were made on May 2, 1910, and reported with optimism and enthusiasm throughout the state. The Meagher County *Republican* printed a special edition dedicated to the "jollification" celebrated by the city's residents. The announcement was certain to put an end to the county seat removal talk that persistently resurfaced even after Castle collapsed. It had most recently been Harlowton that was overtaking the "old city" in importance and population. The WSS & YP would "forever put an end to our town's struggle. We are no longer an inland town."

The newspaper had reported a rumor to the effect that the Milwaukee Company was going to build this railroad, but in this special edition it clarified the facts surrounding its construction.

Lew Penwell, who once lived in White Sulphur Springs and was well aware of its potential, recruited John Ringling and R. M. Calkins of St. Paul, a Milwaukee executive. They were among the prominent out of staters on the board of directors. A station midway between New Dorsey and White Sulphur Springs was named Calkins in honor of the man's efforts on behalf of the new railroad.

Penwell organized yet another company known as the Smith River Development Company. Its plans called for acquiring approximately 250,000 acres of land and selling it to newly arrived settlers when the boom occurred.

The original connection with the Milwaukee was at New Dorsey, but with the reconstruction of the railroad, New Dorsey was bypassed, with Leader becoming the junction point. It boomed beyond expectations, and the city fathers decided to rename it Ringling in a thinly disguised effort to

Tom Coburn collection

Freight on the WSS & YP, 1954.

WSS & YP no. X1162 and cars between Ringling and White Sulphur Springs, 1943.

Warren McGee collection

lure the circus king to make his national headquarters there.

When teased about the abbreviated length of the railroad, its backers replied, "It may not be as long as most others are but it is just as wide as any of them."

Using Milwaukee connections, it was possible to get as close to Yellowstone Park as Gallatin Gateway, where the Milwaukee owned and operated a huge and luxurious hotel. But there was no doubt that the railroad ended at White Sulphur Springs. Several surveys were done extending the line to Cascade on the Missouri River. There were also widely reported hopes that it would replace the stagecoach trail that connected Helena to White Sulphur Springs.

With the completion of the laying of the rails in October of 1910, some five months following its announced beginning, the White Sulphur Springs and Yellowstone Park Railway went into operation.

Its majority shareholder, the Milwaukee, furnished all of its rolling stock and its one locomotive. Successive steam locomo-

tives were brought from Harlowton to pull the combination passenger and freight operations. As time passed, it was observed that the lines in the locomotive that were clogged with scale would clean up with the usage of White Sulphur Springs' pure water. The alkaline condition of water at Harlowton and east of there confounded the condition of steam locomotives. Even following electrification, the Milwaukee would rotate the steam locomotives that ran the abbreviated twenty-three-mile branch to purge the scale from the boilers and steam lines.

The frugal characteristic of management of the WSS & YP soon manifested itself. Every employee sold tickets, shoveled snow, and cleaned the switches. Most of them learned to fire and engineer the locomotive. They did whatever was necessary to bring the freight and passengers to its junction with the transcontinental Olympian and Columbian. The station manager would frequently hire locals to help in shoveling the train out of the snow drifts during the winter months. However, the Milwaukee kept snow equip-

Ron and Cheryl Schrader collection

WSS & YP power, leased from the Milwaukee, 1938.

Warren McGee

ment at Ringling that was used on this line as well as their own right-of-way through the canyon and the summit between the Crazy and Castle mountains.

There were few weeks during the winter when this railroad was free of snow and wind problems. Often the line would be cleared during the day only to blow in during the night. The drifts were sometimes so deep and encrusted that the locomotive would leave the tracks. When this happened, the Milwaukee would dispatch its heavy equipment to the site of the incident and take over the operation.

The railroad was a successful operation during its first few years, but following World War I, the agricultural basis of Montana's economy began to fail. The homestead movement, a brief ten-year experiment, was doomed when it was discovered that the soil of the high plains wasn't the least fertile when it lacked moisture. A long and deep recession followed, with farm credit unavailable and abandonments and tax sales be-

coming the norm throughout the high plains. Commodity prices tumbled, making even well-managed operations marginally profitable even if they were't deeply in debt, which many of them were. The tiny railroad paid a fifteen percent dividend in 1921, its last until 1936. The freight business declined to 6,700 tons in 1932 and revenues dropped to an astonishing $16,000.

Inasmuch as the Milwaukee owned fifty one percent of the stock in the company, they requested abandonment in 1944. Their plea stated that annual tonnage was less than 10,000 tons, that revenue was but $25,000 per year, and there was $40,000 in deferred maintenance that was rapidly coming due. Stockmen, the governor, and both senators from Montana spoke out against the abandonment; and eventually George Weatherall of White Sulphur Springs and W.C. Ramsey of Hannibal, Missouri, bought out the Milwaukee's interest.

The business boomed again commencing in 1946 with the shipping of wood

Meagher County Historical Society

Milwaukee power on the WSS & YP, 1938.

Washout at Moss Agate flats, 1929.

Ron & Cheryl Schrader collection

At the throttle of a WSS & YP locomotive, 1944

Ron and Cheryl Schrader collection

WSS & YP "Galloping Goose", 1952.

Ron & Cheryl Schrader collection

A Milwaukee 4-4-0 on the WSS & YP, 1948.   **Ron & Cheryl Schrader collection**

Ron and Cheryl Schrader collection   **Milwaukee Railroad steam engine, known as "Sagebrush Annie", used on the WSS & YP 1948.**

harvested from nearby mountains. The maintenance program commenced in 1946 and was completed in 1947. Eight miles of rail and bridge timbers were bought from the Milwaukee for the rehabilitation. But unfortunately, the bubble burst in 1954 when tonnage had again declined from a high in 1951 of 153,000 tons to 35,000 tons in 1954. The winter schedule called for one train per week and the passenger service became history. The rail car had been scrapped in 1944 and the steam locomotive followed in 1955. Nicknamed "Sage Brush Annie," the train service between White Sulphur Springs and Ringling became a casualty of better highways and the trucking industry.

A brief interlude of increased tonnage again came to theWSS & YP line when timber harvesting produced wood chips that were carried to Ringling to meet the Milwaukee freight trains for the long haul east. When the Milwaukee bankrupted for the last time in 1980 and discontinued all operations west of Miles City, the only reason for the tiny railroad's existence vanished.

Attempts to breathe life into the line have not met with success, resulting in several vandalized coaches reposing in White Sulphur Springs and a few deteriorating buildings reminding visitors of its heralded past. The rails have been removed and the rotting ties ripped from the soil. A vintage snow plow, once attched to flat bed cars and pushed in front of locomotives, rest sidetracked near the original town site of Dorsey.

The dilapidated depot in White Sulphur Springs was renovated for the movie "Heartland" in 1982, as was the Great Northern coach #902. It had been built in 1904 and spent its last years in the yards at Great Falls until King Wilson had it towed to the "Springs" in hopes of resurrecting a railroad there.

All that remains of the White Sulphur Springs and Yellowstone Park Railway are its memories, in the minds of people like Tom Coburn, the lines engineer. Other memories stir the coals of bitter recall. The

Ron & Cheryl Schrader collection   WSS & YP spur to poleyard, White Sulphur Springs, 1949.

Milwaukee steam engine on the WSS & YP Railroad.   **Tom Coburn collection**

Tom Coburn collection   Fred Coburn with engine no. 42, WSS & YP Railroad, 1955.

WSS & YP combination car, 1925.

Milwaukee diesel power comes to the WSS & YP at Ringling, 1960.

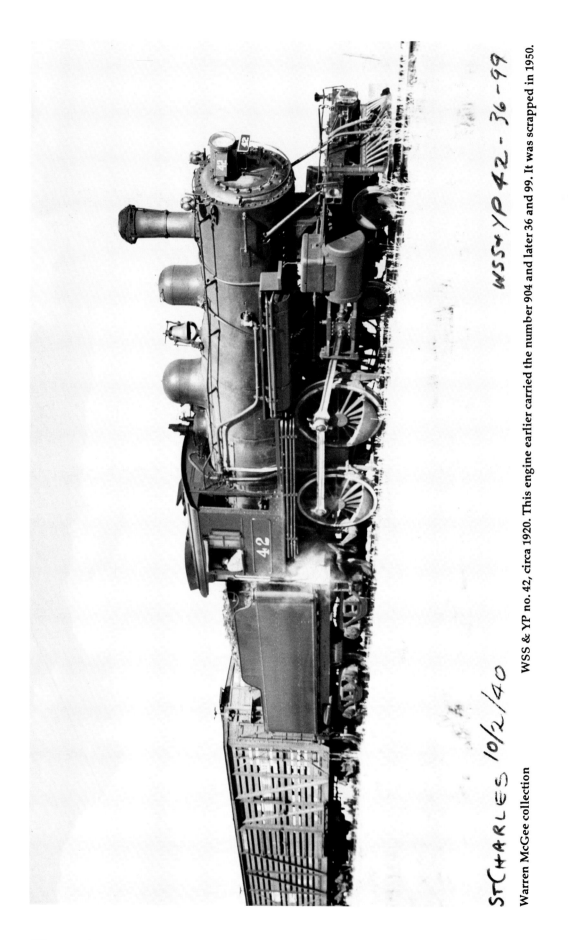

ST CHARLES 10/2/40

WSS+YP 42-36-99

WSS & YP no. 42, circa 1920. This engine earlier carried the number 904 and later 36 and 99. It was scrapped in 1950.

Warren McGee collection

Tickets for a special run by the WSS & YP.

**An excursion with Milwaukee power on
the WSS & YP, 1957.**

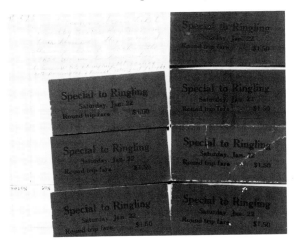

Warren McGee collection

Warren McGee collection

town never did attain the prominence that was predicted for it. The giant tourist complex that was predicted at the turn of the century never materialized, nor did it resurrect itself when this railroad served this town. The mining business collapsed and the for-

est products business has downsized because of enviromnental restrictions, workmen's compensation claims that balloon the cost of carrying the necessary insurance, and the competitive disadvantage of inland transportation.

A recent photo of a WSS & YP snowplow, still on the gound at Canyon Spur, 24 miles from Lombard.

INDEX